THE GIFTS
OF
DESPERATION

A JOURNEY BACK TO ME!

All My Love,

Ocean

2/20/24

OCEAN EAGLE

MINDSTIR MEDIA

Published by Mindstir Media, LLC
45 Lafayette Rd | Suite 181| North Hampton, NH 03862 | USA
1.800.767.0531 | www.mindstirmedia.com

Printed in the United States of America
ISBN-13: 978-1-961532-92-2

A Word from Ocean Eagle

"The level of my healing is directly linked to the depth of My Surrender!" OE

I'm not Buddhist or claim any religion or outside beliefs as I am Not Anything! If I attach to one belief system or modality, I separate myself from the One Thing which is Everything.

Awaken and know you are Somebody, the "Sum of all Bodies", and we are All Gods unlocking our Essence, the Purpose we were born with.

We no longer feel a longing to seek a master, guru or teacher. We embody all of those within our own Being and remember we are information processors. This awareness of Self comes with a great responsibility to shine our truth into this existence and learn how to harness this new found endless Energy.

My classroom is in my chest and I am both Teacher and Student there. Clearing the mind of all thoughts allows me to drop inward where I teach myself based on how my cells react to the frequencies of each message needing discernment.

More and More this process is quicker and quicker. Almost instantly, my inner wisdom guides me with less and less conscious effort as the outdated software that kept me in chains is being dismantled.

Who I did not Trust, was Me! I took ownership of the fact that I called in everything in my life that caused pain and suffering. To develop Love and Trust for my own choices has been an amazing journey. As I feel the vibrations of my cellular temple, I intuitively know truth within for that which used to baffle me.

I no longer struggle and fight......I simply Surrender to a higher frequency that is lovingly guiding ME back to Love of Self.

May You receive The Gifts of Desperation and find the strength and courage to turn inward until you realize You Are Everything You Have Been Searching For.

Now, navigate the Ocean of feelings in your heart and Fly Like an Eagle!

Ocean Eagle

How Desperate Are You?

Do you feel like a drowning man/woman reaching for a life preserver? Are you drowning in a sea of shame, remorse, self-doubt, childhood wounding, trauma, guilt, and low self-esteem?

Are you playing out your past in the now in order to ignore the necessary work needed to rise above it?

Are you trapped in the vicious cycle of PTSD?

Are you unable to connect on a deep level with your daughter or son?

Are you unable to hold, love and protect the feminine/masculine in your life?

Are you unable to set healthy boundaries and hold them?

Are you allowing destructive masculine energy to control you?

Are you unable to look in the mirror and love who you see?

Are you lost in the ocean of this false existence and unable to see a way out?

Are you numbing your feelings with alcohol, drugs, sex, media, food, and other forms of unhealthy behaviors?

Are you stuck in victim mode and justifying your unhealthy behaviors because of the past you feel you didn't deserve?

As a survivor who has become a "Thriver", I learned how to Alchemize my childhood traumas and wounding into a burning flame of Inspiration and Hope for others still suffering. I have deep wisdom in addiction, trauma, and PTSD recovery.

I've been sober from All substances for 23 years and I guide people inward through the natural breath only.

Without the Gifts of Despearation, I might have never been willing to take the necessary inward journey to find my True Self!

THE GIFTS OF DESPERATION
"A JOURNEY BACK TO M.E."

Until I reached the point where I was as desperate as a drowning person reaching for a life preserver, I remained unwilling to do the necessary work to change my reality. It is a constant death and rebirth process that remains a constant in my life now.

Like the serpent, I need to shed the skins that no longer served my highest and best self. This internal/eternal journey and the Alchemical Process of Self Purification are necessary to grow and know and remember who I am!

In order to grow from my poor decisions of the past, I had to understand where they originated and how I was allowing them to control me. I needed to understand what soul contracts were in order to gain awareness and recognize when they had expired.

Why was I constantly trying to hammer a square peg into a round hole it was never meant to fit in? (Relationships, jobs, family, situations, etc.).

I had to learn how to descend
deeper in order to rise higher.

Now awakened, messages are being channeled through me by the Creator (higher self). Sharing my life experiences (wisdom) are a way for the world to relate to and hear the messages more clearly.

As I align my will with the creative forces of the universe, everything makes sense, and once blind, now I see.

> Today, I will help someone rise to their inner greatness by sharing my wisdom and expect nothing in return!

LOOKING IN THE DARK WITHOUT A FLASHLIGHT OR GUIDE! ....

I need the guidance of trusted light/dark workers to navigate the depths of my wounded, traumatized, abandoned, abused, and neglected Soul to bring it out of the dark and into the light.

Finding the right people to guide me through the depths of my wounding was paramount.

I did psycho talk therapy on and off for 15 years as I worked on my inner child wounding. I became familiar with my wounds again and relived them, over and over. The problem was that I wasn't doing anything to transmute them into positive life force energy (inner chi) by healing them.

I was given tools and treatments to help me cope with the feelings and emotions at that moment, but nothing to actually go into the dark with my light from above and shine my light on them, pull them up, and cut the cord of energy I was choosing to give them.

Nicolle and Kadea (trusted light workers) tag-teamed me for 4 years as I remained desperate and willing enough to do the work and assignments I was given.

I wrote (I hated writing at the time, lol), read certain suggested books, and meditated in nature and at home over and over again.

I used to constantly ask God for directions and guidance, but I could not begin communicating with my Creator until I cleared the path of stuck energy from my programmed mind to my Heart. In order to move forward on my healing journey,

I had to stop the "mental ambush" that awaited me at every turn in my life.

I receive crystal clear messages today from my own inner source, and I no longer question them as I know it is no longer my ego tricking me.

I realize revealing and refueling the wounds is not healing!

Today, I choose to remain willing to
go to any lengths to heal!

Living in Acceptance ....

Until I learned to accept everyone and everything exactly as they or it was, I was constantly trying to make the world look the way I needed it to look in order to feed my wounds.

Trying to make sense of the outside world when internally I couldn't make sense of myself was a constant practice in futility.

Nothing ever felt right as I was trying to arrange my outer world to feel happy, safe, loved and complete.

I could never just be still in the moment, and my mind always raced in a thousand directions, taking me places my heart didn't want to go. I wanted to be the puppet master and pretend everyone was on a string that I was controlling. When they wouldn't dance the way I wanted, I was frustrated, angry, and a victim.

Living in a place of acceptance and releasing my expectations has led me to inner peace in all situations. I no longer try to control my environment or other people. That does not mean I have to remain in situations and around people in a passive state.

"I'm not a doormat for others to wipe their wounds on." OE

When I learned how to set healthy boundaries and just move on from others and situations that did not resonate at my frequency, life began to flow effortlessly and with much more peace.

Discernment in all I do is practicing healthy boundaries and validating ME.

I no longer try to control things or people and just bring the best version of me, as I am the only one I have control of.

Today, I accept everything and everyone
for what and who they are!

WALKING INTO A ROOM AS MY TRUTH ....

I used to walk into events and gatherings looking for two things.

Who is my threat, aka the alpha?

Who do I need validation from, aka the prettiest woman?

I needed to see who the Alphas were so I could size myself up to them. I was never enough just showing up as me as I had no idea who I was.

I was just this false ego-masked shell of a human and fake show called Marty Daniel. Inside, I was terrified that I couldn't measure up physically or mentally. If they knew who I really was, they would reject me as I am just a bundle of shame and self-pity with no self-esteem inside. Constantly comparing myself to them and avoiding them at all costs, I always felt less than and not enough.

I also needed to pick out the prettiest woman and stare at her until she made eye contact with me, and then I could release my gaze.

I sought Validation from women all the time, even though I did not have the self-confidence to approach the ones I really wanted to.

My egoic false belief system needed this in order to tell me I was attractive and desired.

I needed to be seen, and that need came from my forsaken child wound. I never felt seen, validated, or appreciated by my parents.

Once I did my work around this, I began to quiet the voice in my head that told me I needed outside validation but I was not worthy.

Before I enter situations, I always pause and create a safety bubble around me and tell myself, "I am enough, and I am loved just as I am"! I no longer care what others think about me, and I just show up as ME. Leading with my heart in all situations, my frequency attracts those I'm meant to connect with. The details are none of my business!

> Today, I walk in the world with my head held high and confident that I am enough as my authentic truth!

GIVE WITH HUMILITY AND NO EXPECTATIONS ....

Man, did I constantly trip on this one?

I used to help people with my time and money, thinking I was doing good deeds. The only problem was, I needed everyone to know what I had done so they would think highly of me.

It was never enough just showing up, doing something nice for someone, and walking away in humble service, and my generosity to others always came with a price tag.

On a small scale, an example of this is when I put tip money in the tip jar at a coffee shop or any place.

I would wait until the employee could see me before dropping the money in the tip jar to get that instant validation ... so silly. My ego needed to know when they counted the tip money, they knew my dollar was part of the final tally.

Once, I knew this family in my church who had been living in a house for years with no flooring. The husband was missing in action, and the mother was barely holding things together. I paid for and installed flooring in their entire house as a gift. That would have been amazing, except that I needed to tell everyone what I had done so they would know I was a good person. I was trying to placate the foresaken child wound that was never seen.

I am valid, just being authentically and truthfully me.

I am my own validator. The blessings from being of service and giving to others come when we don't tell anyone. We allow the energy to flow with no expectations of receiving anything.

"The details are none of my business as the universe takes care of that part." When I receive from others, I often don't even realize it is what I needed all along and it always aligns with my inner guided truth and essence!

Today, I show up in service to the world with no expectations or need for the acknowledgment to stroke my false ego!

Tried to Make the Physical Attraction into Soul Connection/Love ....

How many times did I do this?

What is true for me today is that I know I was always trying to love from an unhealed and abandoned heart.

I was incapable of knowing true love because I didn't love myself. Trying to force love never worked out, and I ignored the red flags one after another when it came to women.

Like me, I was picking women who did not have proper boundaries/discernment and chose to ignore the red flags I presented. I hopped from one relationship to another terrified to be alone. The walls in the house felt like they were closing in around me when I was by myself.

I am 54 years old and have been married three times. Looking back, I never picked a woman that was spiritually healthy and fit.

I was scared and wounded, so I picked women who were likewise scared and wounded. I had to turn inward and create a "New Familiar" one day at a time that was rooted in my own healing.

When we love from our wounds, we can't have true intimacy or trust!

I understand we are all scared to some extent, and today I choose to prioritize my inner calling as number one in my life.

I make deep connections with people these days and live in the nothingness of the Great Mystery of the unknown regarding a relationship.

Having developed a deep inner connection with my Creator, I'm no longer alone and abandoned, as He/She is always with me.

I walk today a free man who no longer wishes he had something others have. I'm happy when I see connected couples in love and no longer feel sorry for myself. Again, the details are none of my business!

Today, I will develop trust and love with others based on a heart-centered connection!

Trying to Force a Square Peg into a Round Hole ....

If it doesn't fit, it doesn't fit.

It's not my job to try and shape someone or myself into something neither is it to make a relationship work.

It does not matter how amazing she is on the outside; the relationship either vibrates at similar frequencies, or it doesn't.

I no longer make concessions or give up who I am to appease anyone. If two people can't go into the mixing bowl and come out tasting good without having to add or take away from one another, then it's not going to work or at the very least become a struggle.

When I give up a part of me I loved, or vice versa, it eventually becomes a resentment or weapon when times are difficult.

"How can you say that or act like that? ...."

"Don't you know what I've sacrificed for you?".

I should say instead, "Don't you know what I have CHOSEN to sacrifice for you?" Arguments would happen when my relationship wasn't going the way I thought it should, or I wasn't getting my way.

It's MY Fault if I choose to sacrifice myself in any way to make the relationship work.

It's always an inward turn as I focus on my part only.

I no longer try to save something I know will never serve my highest and best good. For me, the old way of saying relationships are hard and complicated or there are sacrifices to be made does not resonate with me.

It either works, or it doesn't work.

If it is not working, I look at myself and ask why I chose this person in the first place. I see where I had ignored parts of my partner because I really wanted someone in my life and not because I truly loved all of her.

> Today, I know the person meant to be next to me will show up when the Creator is ready for her to show up.

I Focus on Bringing More Love to this World as I am in Service to my Creator's Will ....

I am no longer looking for love to be happy and valid.

To me, the highest and most powerful universal force is Love! That is why we crave it so profoundly.

Call it love or anything you wish, but to me, it's the feeling of being seen in your true naked form, feeling safe and held void of all judgments. The gift of knowing how to give it to myself and filling my own cup has been paramount for my growth.

When I knew I was enough just as I was and didn't need to change my innermost being, I cannot describe the emotions that poured out within me. My essence was intact all along, and I just needed the key of self awareness that unlocked the cage it was hidden in.

Once unlocked, Divine Shakti coursed through my body like nothing I've ever felt.

To be a vessel for the Creator in this world and guide others home so they can experience pure love is my life's purpose now.

I will let others know that a poor wretch like me dug his way out of the depths of pain and suffering and stands upright before the world without apologizing for who he is today.

I will share because I deeply care about all humans and pray we all awaken the truth that lies within.

> Today, I will walk my talk and spread
> love everywhere spirit leads me!

GIVING UNSOLICITED OPINIONS
AND FREE ADVICE ....

I'll ask for your opinion if I want it, and that goes both ways.

I try not to give unsolicited free advice.

When I do this, I say your perception is wrong or needs to be adjusted, as if I know your truth.

When I begin acting like your Guru, I become a know-it-all, and I am playing God.

Your perception and truth are Yours and none of my business.

I needed to learn how to meet people where they were in life and bring Love and Compassion.

I feel that I'm still working on this one and always will be.

To some extent, we all judge, and I believe some judgments are healthy discernments that keeps us at arm's length from unhealthy people. When others explain why the way I see things is wrong, without me asking, I simply try to ignore it and move on. Ultimately, we all learn through our own experiences and not what we read or are told. Otherwise, we are made up of others' views and ideas and never develop our own authentic truth.

Now that I have stepped out of the dream and woken up, I desperately want to rid myself of the unhealthy judgment of my brothers and sisters.

When I judge, it's always about my own flaws and has nothing to do with you.

The inner calmness and peace within me, allows me to be free of most judgments I allowed to poison ME.

Again, always making an inward turn if I want to grow and be free of the chains binding me to unnecessary struggles and suffering.

> Today, I will offer advice when asked or ask permission before I do, as I validate your perceptions and feelings!

WHEN ASKED, I JUST DELIVER MY PERCEPTION/TRUTH WITH NO ATTACHMENT TO HOW IT IS RECEIVED ....

I don't want to volunteer information appearing like a Guru, Master, or like I have your answers ....

I speak my truth and release how it is received.

My truth and authenticity are ever-evolving based on my experiences and the information I gather that I take to the classroom within my chest. I offer my advice or my opinion from a thoughtful, authentic, and truthful place when anyone asks me for it.

I do not say what people want to hear as I have nothing I'm trying to sell them. Sometimes the truth hurts and people do not want to hear it, but I don't soft-shoe how I feel when asked.

Many people want their issues or problems to be solved. If I do not have experience regarding their problem, I say, "I can't help you with that issue as I have no experience with it."

I feel teachers and coaches trying to make a living guiding others feel like they have to say something because they are being paid to do so.

Whether I'm being paid or not, I will always say my truth, and if it does not resonate with you, that is fine.

I have no attachment or expectation on how anything I share will be received.

This book may not sell a single copy, and I'll be ok.

It's not for everyone!

No gurus, no masters, no teachers, and that means ME.

Today, I only have love, compassion, and my
wisdom which is gleened from my experiences!

THOUSANDS OF YEARS OF GENERATIONAL PROGRAMMING TO UNWIND ....

The generational hard wiring and trapped energy passed down on both sides of my family shaped my belief system. I am unwinding and unbinding myself from those patterns and belief systems one day at a time. Years ago I was in a year-long men's trauma and addiction recovery group and each person was asked to do what they called a Trauma Egg. It was a large, white artboard, and we were to draw the shape of an egg on it. Within the egg, we were to draw small picture windows and inside each picture window we were to draw a scene or something that would remind us of trauma events in our life. When we each presented our eggs, the other guys in the group had between 12-20 traumas, respectively. When my turn came, you could have heard a pin drop as they sucked all the air out of the room. My egg had 123 picture windows of stick figure drawings of the traumas I could remember.

That was just the traumas from this incarnation and for me only. Imagine how much heavy energy and wounding must be restored to heal the generational lineage hardwiring stored in our DNA. My father had four brothers and sisters, and my mother had the same. Dysfunctional behavior, mental issues, and addiction ran deep on both sides. My mother and father were products of their own hardwiring and damage created during their upbringing. My father died a physically, mentally, financially, and spiritually broken man 14 years ago. I remember him telling me that he felt like he had nothing to offer anyone after losing his company due to his poor decisions. Of course, he was so sad and had a massive pity party for himself as he wallowed in the depths of sadness, remorse, and self-loathing. I look back now at that conversation with love and compassion for him. I don't judge his life anymore as his path was designed for him. I actually needed him to be who he was in my life for me to be who I am today. Gratitude is such a blessing to possess.

Today, I'm always willing to work on healing my lineage!

Wasted Time Planning ....

I no longer plan anything that is not necessary.

Of course, I need to make travel arrangements for places I'm going and events I'm invited to, but I leave it to the Universal Frequency Matrix where this path is leading me.

I had plans to attend 5 different events in 5 different countries in 2020, and some had non-refundable deposits at risk. I was looking forward to these trips, but deep inside, I knew my ego was involved.

Spirit spoke loud and clear to me through my inner voice, saying, "surrender to the unknown, and you will be guided."

When I surrendered my will and changed my plans, massive confirmations came in immediately letting me know I had aligned my will with my inner truth.

If I'm truly an open channel for the creator to work through, He has already arranged the details.

I just need to stay open, willing, and constantly surrender to that force.

I make plans but I do not become attached to them. I'm always open to change.

I believe everything and everyone coming into my field is meant to be here. I'm no longer calling in lessons by attracting humans not meant to be in my life.

There is no more wasted time daydreaming of what might be and take right action instead.

I stay present in each moment, so I don't miss the magic.

My favorite thing to do is wake up because I know something amazing will happen.

I don't know many who can say that. Most feel trapped in the existence they have created to feel safe, and there is no room to just let go and receive the divine messages they ignore daily.

> Today, I don't attach to any plans, and I
> LET GO and TRUST ABSOLUTELY!

I Stopped Playing God ....

I don't play God to myself or others.

I do not have anyone's answers or solutions to their problems.

I meditate, get still and turn inward for my truth and answers only.

They come when I am supposed to receive them and not when I try to strangle them out of this existence.

Much of the time, my truths and answers come spontaneously without effort. I no longer drink the Kool-Aid society, cultures and governments have offered as truth without investigating what's in it.

I no longer accept the words of others at face value just because that person is well known, famous or in a position of perceived power.

When I can feel my way through life's situations and decisions, I don't have stress, and I'm not anxious. I have stopped numbing my feelings and sit with them in silence as they don't scare me anymore.

As for others in my life, I only share my experience, strength, and hope.

I share from experience based on what happened in my life (wisdom).

I share my strength, or what I did, to unlock my heart and soul so that I could become my own teacher (willingness).

I share my hope that people will begin to understand the answers they seek are buried deep within, under years of wounding, trauma, and suffering (winning).

Wounding and suffering others are choosing to keep alive control them as they continue to give their power to the old story.

Wounding
Wisdom
Willingness
Winning

Today, I will not play God and keep my ego
in check in order to share my wisdom!

DON'T CONTROL OR MANIPULATE THE OUTCOME ....

This life is about the non-attachment to outcomes and results for me. Learning to be void of expectations has set me free and I simply focus on bringing the best version of me to all I do.

I do the work and trust the outcome will be what it's meant to be.

I put the best ME into everything I choose to do and then sit back and let the outcome unfold.

I can always live with the outcome
if I have done my best.

When my heart is in it before earthly wants or desires, the end result will be as it should be and None of My Business.

But if I commit to something and know I didn't give it all I had, no matter the results, I always feel like it could have been better.

However, when I try to force the outcome, everyone involved suffers, and it never ends well.

Trying to bully my way through people and life to get what I want pushes people away and what I end up with never feels right, no matter the outcome. This is often one of the best times to practice self-love and compassion as I acknowledge my humanness and selfishness. I commit to doing better next time and avoid the pitfalls of trying to control situations and humans.

Today, I understand when things do not go the way I would have them, it is a blessing in disguise to be revealed in time.

What and Who are You Attached to that Does Not Serve Your Highest and Best Potential? ....

If your answer is not "I am my own master," I encourage you to clear away all lower vibrational people and things blocking you from the divine light and energy within YOU!

I've cleared away the dead weight that wasn't serving my highest and best self. I cleared away relationships with friends and family whose energies pulled me down.

People ask me, "how did you walk away from family members?" Easy, blood, no blood, makes no difference to me.

Society keeps us anchored to people in our families that are toxic for us to be around because we feel we owe them something. Once I understood I owed no one anything, I was free to release all toxicity blocking my higher calling.

I have had a profound experience of Oneness with All on this planet.

I'm closer with people I've known for less than 36 months than anyone in my previous 50 years because I am setting proper boundaries.

Not because I'm programmed to believe just because I was born into a family, I have to spend time with them or allow their heavy energy into my life. There are people in life I have to love from afar.

I'm building a family of my choice today, and I owe nothing to anyone! I now serve my call to love, evolve to my true purpose and follow my divine inner light.

I can't take dead weight with me when I leave this incarnation, so why drag it around while I'm here?

Today, I say yes to boundaries that serve
my highest and best purpose ... ME!

I CAN'T LEAD OTHERS TO A PLACE OF INNER HEALING WITHOUT LOVE AND COMPASSION FOR MYSELF FIRST! ....

I will continue to preach that I cannot give away what I do not possess.

If I don't love myself first and have compassion within, I cannot expect to give them away in a healthy way. I spent half a lifetime living this false existence and loving from an empty cup, my wounds.

I have love and compassion for others based on how deeply I love myself.

Otherwise, I make up some version of love I think you need that is not authentic and based on my past wounding.

People can feel it when it is not authentic, and I lose my credibility in friendships and relationships.

The relationship becomes false, and I have to keep trying to love them when I don't or save something already gone because I was attached to it.

I love others with good intentions, but well short of how I'm capable of loving them as I am always working on loving myself on a deeper level. Until self-love is acquired, I have no business attempting to love another.

Years of a programmed and wounded existence will not go away overnight, and the road Home requires patience if I truly learn how to fill my cup.

Love is the answer, so once I've achieved self-love, I'll have the answer I've longed to find.

> Today, self-love, compassion, and patience are the code.

USING MY STORY TO BE
SELF-DESTRUCTIVE ....

I was a walking poster of a child who was a victim and always felt sorry for my sorry ass.

Rationalizing and justifying my self-destructive behaviors, left me imprisoned by my childhood and teenage traumas/wounds.

My past was a huge crutch that could never support the weight of self-pity I carried.

I was a human wrecking ball. Everything was about me as I tried to mask my wounds with unhealthy behavior, women, alcohol, drugs, and self-sabotage.

I would tell anyone who would listen to my sad tale for them to feel sorry for me and, therefore, love and accept me.

My self-esteem was so low that I thought my old story was all I had to offer.

Whenever I did something that would create a severe consequence, I always played the victim role or just accepted it because it aligned with the familiar feelings of childhood.

I had excuses ready to pull out of my pocket for everything. It was just the fact that I got caught or If I had left the party 10 minutes earlier I would not be sitting in this jail cell.

I had No idea what ownership was so I constantly blamed my childhood or someone else for my problems.

Ownership is the first step to recovery, and I had to be honest with myself and the world around me. We are only as sick as the secrets of our past so when I share them with someone I trust, I'm no longer alone with them. Secrets keep you constantly looking over your shoulder for the boogeyman when the real boogeyman is YOU!

Today, I will no longer use my past to justify my present!

FAITH WITHOUT WORK DIES ....

If I do not surrender and trust the creator knows what's best for me, I start feeling like I want to control things.

I then expect things to magically happen the way I want them to.

I feel I'm owed the job.
I'm owed that girlfriend or wife.
I'm owed a larger bank account.
I'm owed nicer clothes.
I'm owed a better car.
I'm owed more time off.
I'm owed, I'm owed, and I'm owed.

I have to trust and have complete FAITH that everything is exactly as it should be and do the necessary work I commit to doing.

I must do the daily work required to keep that faith wide open and unwavering. I do this with SALT ....

Surrender, Accept, Let Go, and Trust on a daily basis.

I can quickly feel when I'm off these days and right the ship through meditation and mindful Feeling.

I'm also kind, compassionate, and loving to myself as I accept my humanness.

When things don't go as planned, I look at my part and ask if I did enough and where I can improve.

If I feel complete with my efforts, I trust God had a hand in the outcome and let it go.

If I fall short of doing my best, I acknowledge it and move on without shaming myself.

Today, I will faithfully do what needs to be done to keep the communication with the Creator wide open.

MY PERSONAL POWER IS NO LONGER SCATTERED IN THE OLD STORY ....

Through many years of working with my Spirit Guides, Nicolle and Kadea, I was able to label my traumas, abandonments, abuses, and neglects one by one.

I am now validating each of them and no longer brushing them under the rug by saying things like, "Other kids in the world had it worse than me."

I Am Valid, and What Happened Sucked ... Period!

I had to reveal and re-feel them before I could heal them.

It was necessary to feel them again in order to let them go.

By labeling them, I understood that I had sent out a cord to each one containing a portion of my personal power.

Eventually, I became powerless, as all of my power was in the old story and I kept using it to justify why my life sucked or why I continued to abuse drugs and alcohol.

I was a "seemingly" hopeless victim.

I say seemingly because it was all in my head ... a made-up version of me to keep me safe so I didn't have to feel anymore.

My false 'ego mask' kept me alive during tough times, and today, I am grateful for that version of myself that no longer serves me.

I have so much love, compassion, and gratitude for my ego mask that kept the air moving in and out of my lungs.

How we each heal our wounds is a personal journey to find a path that works for us.

Everyone learns and heals differently, and I encourage opting for different guides and teachings until you find the one that best suits you and aligns with your frequency and vibrational field.

Today, I choose to no longer feed my
old story with my energy!

No More "I'm Sorry" ....

I'm not a sorry person!

Words have inner meanings and values I've attached to them, so I have to be mindful of how I use them.

Saying "I'm Sorry" has become a part of how people communicate and inner programming.

I used to say that phrase without understanding that it was hardly necessary.

I prefer to say "excuse me" or "pardon me" in many situations where I used to randomly say "I'm sorry."

There is rarely a reason to call myself sorry or even say I'm sorry as I do my best to make choices from a place of Love.

I acknowledge accidents happen all the time, but I prefer to say "I feel sad" about what happened. If my actions created or added to an outcome that hurts someone, I make an effort to right my wrong through action and not some bailout meaningless phrase humanity has adopted. There is a reason they call creating words "spelling." The meanings the mysterious world assigns to them actually cast a 'Spell' on you energetically. You don't even know you are shaming yourself.

Changing my verbiage helps change my vibrational frequency. I simply walk and stand in truth from a place of authentic love. There is never a reason to be sorry for that.

> Today, I will be more mindful of when I owe an apology and not shame myself with my own verbiage.

Learning to Not Sweat the Small Stuff or Big Stuff ....

If someone gets upset (and I'm no different) over spilled milk or food, they are acting like they have never done it.

Who has not spilled food or a drink? We all have!

I have been the worst in the past with my kids.

I'm sure they may need a Spirit Guide someday to help them navigate some of the emotional woundings I created as they were growing up.

Driving is a beautiful place to practice this on a daily basis.

I can decide to stay calm and peaceful when someone cuts me off, or I can flip them the middle finger as I kindly show them where God lives.

I have a choice to give my personal energy away in each situation, poisoning myself with toxic feelings or just release it immediately through a deep breath and let it go!

The other driver does not care and can't hear me when I'm yelling at them, so what is it really about?

For me, it's about expecting the world to line up with how I would do things. It's as if my subconscious mind believes that person woke up that day and said, "I'm going to ruin Ocean's Day and cut him off on the freeway on purpose when I see his car coming."

It is truly a narcissistic way of living as I think it's all about me.

I was walking through life, taking the world's inventory.

Once I realized this, I could turn the finger I was pointing at the world back at myself. This is about me, but not from the seat of the victim. What about me needs to control the world? What about me is in fear around these trivial things in life?

When I choose peace and calm, I am happier and more relaxed in any situation. I take deep breaths before I react to life and I'm soul grateful for the pauses I give myself in life.

> Today, I will Choose to not Sweat the Small (or Big) Stuff and remain peaceful within!

MY TRUTH HAS BECOME A GUIDE FOR LIVING ....

I was forever transformed once my truth was revealed to me, and I saw the essence of my soul's divine purpose.

Ignoring it now would be like starving myself.

I need to follow this path like I physically need food and water to survive.

As I continue to develop my inner relationship with the Creator, everything I thought I wanted has changed.

I no longer want to follow a programmed path the world says I should follow.

When I do this, I go against my heart's desire and passions, and I constantly feel a sense of stress and anxiety.

My path is unique, and my calling from within directs me.

When an opportunity arises, I send it to my chest and ask the Creator if this is the direction I should go. My chest is my classroom, and I become both teacher and student.

Having opened the channel to receive instructions, I'm almost always given an answer, and if not, I take no action and just observe.

If it aligns with service to the world, it's almost always the right path, but sometimes darkness hides in the light, so I have to discern from within.

Someone asked Jesus, "How will I know it's Not You when the adversary shows up?" Jesus replied, "You will know because it will look just like me and talk just like me!"

That is why I believe the wolf will hide in sheep's clothing.

Bringing people and situations into my heart helps me to decide if it or they belong in my life as I trust my inner knowledge now.

I can't imagine not being ME, and I would never have said that before I met myself.

Today, I am soul grateful to have an intimate relationship with the still, small voice within.

A WALKER BETWEEN WORLDS ....

I now understand what walking between the above and the below means.

I live in the middle of the upper and lower worlds and daily journeys into both.

No dark without light and no light without darkness.

It's a relationship of reciprocity and duality, "Ayni," as they say in Peru.

One who has woken up from the dreamlife begins to feel the light and power of the Creator.

However, if all I do is try to walk this planet in the light only, I become separated from the whole, and I no longer feel compassion for others. I'm no longer relatable or able to connect with others. Being human is just as important as being a light warrior.

When I stay in the light, I feel superior somehow and judge others for not having what I have.

People cannot relate to me, and I become too much for them to handle as I appear like I feel I am better than they are.

Staying humble and the right size is so important if I am going to be of maximum service to people. Sharing my story and experiences is the glue and attractive resonance necessary to bond with others and create safety. If others cannot relate to where I've been and what I've experienced, they can't trust me to guide them towards their own healing path.

> Today, I will meet and accept people where they are in life and remain relatable in order to deliver the message of Hope from a place of true love and compassion.

THE CREATIVE UNIVERSAL POWERS ARE WATCHING AND WAITING TO GUIDE YOU TO YOUR ESSENCE AND TRUE PURPOSE ....

I believe the Creator waits for His/Her children to wake up and open to the Divine Energy/Light placed within all of us.

It's not reserved for a particular group, race, sex, or gender ... it's accessible to us all.

But I had to clear away All that was blocking me from opening and surrendering to the Call in my chest. For some, the call comes slowly over time, but for me, I was blown apart in an instant.

My love for all humans and this planet is endless as the expansion I felt in my heart stirred and woke my soul.

In order to be ready for such an event required unloading all of the baggage I was carrying around, which meant doing the necessary things to reveal, re-feel, and heal my wounds from this incarnation and past ones. Once again, I dropped to my knees, surrendered, and didn't question what my guides suggested I do. I knew in my chest I needed to keep diving deeper and deeper if I genuinely wanted to be set free from the soul prison I was stuck in.

When I began doing my inner work, I didn't even know I wanted what I have today. I did not like what I had before and was given The Gift of Desperation to remove all that was blocking and holding me back.

Sometimes Knowing What I Don't Want, Leads Me to What I'm Meant to Have!

Today, I remain open to the unknown possibilities the Creator wants me to receive!

THERE ARE NO BLUEPRINTS ON THE EXTERNAL TO TELL ME WHO I AM OR WHO I'M MEANT TO BE ....

Like reading an earthly blueprint, I had to train myself how to read the one coded within my DNA before I could begin building ME. Architects study and train for years to gain the ability to read a blueprint. This journey of building M.E. was no different.

That meant learning how to trust my intuition and gut as I navigated the blueprint designed specifically for Me and residing inside my cells, DNA, quanta, vibrations, frequencies, heart, and soul.

Once I learned how to unlock my truth/purpose based on the blueprint within, everything started making sense and falling into place effortlessly.

I no longer need to struggle to get what I need to fulfill my purpose in life.

Conversely, the flow of Divine Creation began giving me what I was always meant to have, and it is infinite.

My heart began teaching me who I was meant to be.

Breaking the old habits of going against my inner knowing took time and lots of self-compassion.

It wasn't going away overnight, so patience was also necessary. I've stumbled into old patterns many times on the path home, but the lessons are learned quicker and quicker as my Awareness became much more acute.

Once I was able to clear my mind, I could then begin to meditate on a deeper level and access my blueprint's designs for me.

My inner codes have enabled me to heal enough to move forward in my evolutionary process.

Healing for me requires quiet, time alone, being fearless, sitting in nature, and paying attention to my heart's voice. I simply do not question the still small voice within, no matter how much it goes against the programmed narrative in my mind.

Today I will follow my intuition, my inner voice, and the designs of my inner blueprint!

By Not Honoring My Truth Out of Fear or False Responsibility for Others' Feelings, I Don't Honor ME ....

It all starts with ME!

I have to always Honor myself and my essence (ME). Filling my cup first is the only way I can authentically offer love to others.

Otherwise, I begin making sacrifices and compromises to appease others, and physiologically, my cells know I am not being true to myself. I create my own anxiety, frustration, and fears by saying Yes when my inner voice says No.

I become a fraud to myself, and my soul does not trust me.... I don't trust myself. My inner child does not feel safe again and goes into hiding, so I stop playing and laughing.

When I set my boundaries and honor them, I feel Safe, Happy, Self-Supported, Self-Loved, and Self-Validated.

I no longer need any of that from an external source as I possess it within.

I no longer people, please!

I no longer feel responsible for how others are going to see me.

I walk in my truth, and how you perceive my truth is none of my business.

I am ME, and I don't care what you think about ME because I know my heart intimately now. Those who can't see ME and judge ME will fall away as I remain true to myself. I don't need to do anything; they just leave, and the room is created for the ones to enter who will lift me up.

When I serve ME first, I validate ME, and everyone in my life will be blessed, even if they can't see it!

> Today, I honor, love, and respect ME by calling in all I'm meant to receive through heart-centered vibrations and frequencies.

LEAN IN! I CAN HOLD YOU UNTIL YOU LEARN HOW TO HOLD YOURSELF....

Learning how to hold space for others has been such a beautiful experience.

Listening and creating a safe container of non-judgment allows a space for others to open up and reveal their wounds and fears.

Not offering free advice and trying to fix them is important during this process.

When safety has been created, the opportunity for growth is ushered in, and people begin seeing a way out.

I share my experiences only so others gain Hope that they can find their light within as I have found mine.

I always feel like it is such an honor and blessing to love and support another soul in this way. Many have held sacred space for me on my path, and I would not be who I am today without loving support.

Holding space for another does not mean I enable them.

When it feels like others are becoming dependent on me, it's time to set them free.

If I don't, they will never be willing to begin their journey to find their truth and understand that they, themselves, are the answer they seek. I use my light to light the path, but everyone has to walk it themselves.

No one can have my light; my light is designed for Me specifically and will not show you the steps of the path you must walk.

I believe your path is already within you, and your light is waiting to shine and show you the way home.

Today, I will hold a loving, safe, and sacred space for God's children with reverence and love!

REST AND KNOW THE DIVINITY YOU SEEK LIES WITHIN YOU ....

Nothing externally could open the door to the Divinity within me.

When I say rest, I mean I had to relax and take everything easy.

When my brain goes off and my thoughts are racing, I cannot feel anything in my heart and soul.

I had to learn how to slow my thoughts down (monkey brain) through meditation and by being quiet within.

I accomplished this by really watching the show my brain puts on every day from the seat of the observer. I actually take life breaks and enter the dark, quiet space in the back of my brain. I sit there and watch the show the frontal lobe is performing. I quickly dismiss all thoughts and release them.

It can be exhausting to keep up with everything going on there. I noticed the crazy and insane thoughts that came in and knew it was the conditioning and programming talking, not my heart.

I realize today I am Not responsible for the first thought, but I am responsible for what I do with that thought. By removing these thoughts that do not serve me, I expand the channel from my crown chakra to the classroom in my chest.

In meditation (I will share a few I do later in the book), I can actually stop the incoming thoughts, and I'm able to drop into my Hearts Center to feel my way through life.

Then, the Divine Being I am can be accessed and open communication with my higher self takes place. The feelings and intuition are often immediate and profoundly moving.

> Today, I will feel my way through life through quiet meditation, opening the channel to the Divine Within!

Thank You for Breaking My Heart Over and Over Again to Make More Room for Growth ....

Every heartbreak was necessary to finally become willing to deeply dive into ME.

When relationships were failing, I was always so hard on myself. I was such a martyr hanging on the cross.

Everything happening had to be my fault, so I would break my back doing more and more to make her happy so she wouldn't leave or reject me. Much of this came from my childhood abandonment and the forsaken child wounding.

Deep suffering opens the possibility for Growth and Expansion.

I became tired of the self-inflicted pain and suffering I created by making unhealthy choices in partners.

I had to own my part Only and understand my Soul was calling in all of this pain to get me to my knees. Until I had an awareness of my subconscious beliefs, I could not learn the lessons.

My soul's call kept hammering me over and over again until I became willing to do the inner work necessary to learn the lessons. I needed to become my own teacher and become teachable to clear the way for my light to shine through.

I was destined to keep picking unhealthy, wounded women because it was easier than working on myself. My experience is that humans don't want to do their own work, so they pick partners with the same or similar wounding and try to save or fix them.

Today I am thankful for healthy discernment and honest communication with the women I date. I set clear boundaries, and I'm transparent as I no longer Need love or companionship.

I no longer move the boundaries I have set, and this Honors M.E.

Today, I remain grateful for challenging times as I know there is always a silver lining behind the suffering.

THIS IS A JOURNEY TO THE CENTER OF THE SOUL ....

When I saw my body and spirit as microcosms of the universe, I understood this is a journey to the center of the universe/soul.

The center of my soul sends out the signals/instructions to the surrounding universe giving instructions and creating order out of chaos.

I used to steal the signals or instructions from everything surrounding me, which created chaos within.

It had to be reversed, or I would have kept living my life based on others' ideas, perceptions, and beliefs or false frequencies not meant for ME.

Why would I allow myself to absorb the energies of other existences? Why would I want to attach to others' suffering and generational wounding when I hadn't learned how to deal with or heal myself?

I've got plenty to work on here at home!

Piling on my suffering with the outside suffering of the world blocks me from seeing what I need to work on.

I feel I did this to hide behind the suffering of others, not to have to feel or look at my own.

Self-awareness was key for me to wake up and smell the coffee, so to speak.

When I was able to understand that I needed to be self-centered toward my universal inner healing, I was able to commit to myself on a deeper level. The dark depths were no longer sacred to me and were more accessible with every healing step I was willing to take.

Today, I understand that diving deeper into my
Soul is to dive deeper into discovering ME.

I AM THE MEDICINE ....

I have the medicine within to heal myself and transmute unhealthy feelings, thoughts, habits, addictions, physical ailments, and spiritual maladies.

I used to have debilitating Fear and Anxiety and even had prescribed medication on hand after a nervous breakdown when I was 41 years old. A massive panic attack overtook my body as all of the balls I was juggling crashed to the ground.

Today I have no need for any outside medications.

My medicine today is inner stillness, quietness, self-awareness, and self-love. When I meditate and stop the mind from thinking for my heart/soul, I can receive the messages from Divine Source.

I can take a journey through my own breathing and ask the Creator direct questions believing I will receive the answers immediately or through future alignments and synchronicities.

The key for me is to open the channel to receive and be aware/mindful of who and/or what is coming into my field.

Then I need to be willing to take action by opening up to that person, place, or thing being offered, even if I can't see why I should. Daily S.A.L.T. is required.

There are no accidents for me anymore, no coincidences.

The first time I physically healed myself, I had fire walked 3 times that night. I was lying in bed in my hotel room, and my feet were on fire and scorched red. No one had ever taught me how to heal myself. I simply closed my eyes, focused on my third eye, sent everything I had to my feet, and stated, "heal my feet and allow me to wake with no pain and no blisters." In short order, I fell asleep, and upon waking the following day, my feet were completely healed without a mark anywhere and void of any pain.

When I learned how to self-heal, I was free from feeling I needed something or someone to fix me.

Today, I will Heal myself from within
whenever I need to do so!

BUY A ONE-WAY TICKET HOME; YOU'VE BEEN GONE WAY TOO LONG ....

Time to go home!

Having my heart blown open and having my truth revealed to me was something that opened a whole new world to me.

When I decided to follow my truth without fear of what others would think, it felt like I was finally going Home.

I had never felt like I was home anywhere, not even in the homes I owned in my marriages.

By age 30, I had lived in over 100 houses and apartments, so I never developed roots, and I never knew what that felt like.

Today, no matter where I am, I am always at home within myself. So home is always where my heart is.

That is why I can now travel and not feel alone or abandoned as I bring Home (my heart) with me. In the past, I was constantly running away from my problems, but the problem was Me. I am always the common denominator in all things, and I now run to ME and not away from me.

When I want to feel held,

I meditate and call in the mother's embrace

feeling held by her divine Love and Grace.

The father in my life today is the masculine divine source who holds the parts of me that weren't held by my earthly father.

My forsaken child is no longer screaming to be seen or validated by his earth parents.

When I turned over my will to serve my brothers and sisters, my Divine Parents began blessing me beyond measure. I'm loved, seen, and valid always, and I'm finally home.

> Today, my heart is always with me, so today, I am always home, no matter where I physically exist.

I Am My Answer ....

Today I Am the Great I Am I Always Sought in the World.

I had not developed a relationship with my heart and soul.

The only Me I knew was the outward, earthly projections of my False Ego Mask that kept me on life support until I was ready to learn the lessons my soul came here to learn and heal the wounds it came here to heal.

After my awakening, I understood that nobody and nothing had my answers.

The answers I was always seeking were permanently embedded deep within my own heart, soul, and DNA.

Life's experiences had built barriers blocking me from being able to access all I was given by the Creator to heal myself.

When I feel stress, fear, hurt, or anxiety, I turn inward and get quiet until I realize what the energy is (the feeling), recognize where the energy is coming from (what wound), and have an immediate reckoning (power grab) with that wound as I no longer allow it to have my power and control me.

My feelings are always about me, so it is my responsibility to love, care for, correct, and heal ME from within.

When I am feeling hurt, sad, and angry, I know there is something about me that sets the stage somehow. What choices had I made that set me up for this life lesson? What boundary did I move because of unhealthy desires? What had I ignored to get 'My Way'?

It's my job to be willing to be my own answer and be willing to suffer if I'm not willing to take the necessary steps.

I am, and I always was the answer I was looking for.

> Today, I look no further than my mirror
> at home for my answers!

FALSE BELIEFS WERE FED TO ME THROUGH FAMILY, FRIENDS, TEACHERS, RELIGION, CULTURE, AND LIFE'S EXPERIENCES ON THE LINEAR PLANE, KEEPING ME STUCK IN A FALSE REALITY ....

I realized my belief system and thought patterns were not mine.

The False Beliefs and Deals I made based on outside influences were just coping mechanisms so my system could make sense of the chaos that was my life.

Every new trauma, abandonment, neglect, and abuse would receive a new agreement that I would then live by.

For example, at age 8, saying, "I'm never getting married".

I began negotiating with life to survive and hide/mask my pain.

Later, alcohol, drugs, and women would become ways to cope with my PTSD, pain, non-existent self-esteem, fear, and abandonment issues.

With all that took place, my little boy and the young man could not deal with life on life's terms, so I needed my own set of terms to keep me alive.

Once awake, it became obvious that I did not have many original thoughts or ideas, if any.

At age 50, I found myself wanting to undo All I thought I knew because everything I lived by led me to pain and suffering.

I craved a new way of life that was authentically mine, so I began the process of starting a new book of life.

I even started to try and write with my off-hand, drive with my off-hand, drive on the wrong side of the road, run on the left side of trails, and eat/drink with my opposite hand. The system had to be burned to the ground.

I needed a new book that was all mine and one I could truly trust and believe in.

The new book of Marty Ocean Eagle Daniel is soul much fun to write as I have zero limiting beliefs anymore.

Today, I am the author of my new reality!

I Kept Trying to Have Relationships with Other Unhealed Souls/Humans ....

Never feeling good enough to choose a healthy partner, I always picked women who "I thought needed saving."

It wasn't that they asked to be saved. I chose to see them needing saving, so I would put on my Superman cape and fly in to save the day. Me? Mr. Broken and Wounded?

When I look back at my part, I clearly see I never loved anyone from a healthy, healed heart.

At age 50, I realized I had never loved anyone from a place deep in my heart it was closed off.

That deeper place was revealed to me through an intimate connection with a woman I shared sacred space with recently.

She opened a place in my heart I didn't know existed, and it is a gift I will always cherish.

I loved from my wounded heart, so the relationships were always doomed from the beginning, no matter how long they lasted on codependency and deal-making life support.

I felt if I just loved them enough and made them happy, everything would be okay. I allowed them to be narcissistic victims and addicts.

My love was going to be enough to keep it all together.... Not!

My truth today is I'm not ready for a committed relationship as my calling continues to manifest and I get to know ME.

In recent relationships, I've tripped over old patterns and behaviors that in the past would have pulled me in for years, but I get quicker and quicker at realizing, recognizing, and having a reckoning with each stumble. I own my part, see where I need growth, and give myself love and compassion as I traverse the slippery slope of love, lust, and physical attraction.

> Today, I no longer look for nor need to be loved by someone to feel safe and happy.

> **ONCE MY TRUE HEART AND SOUL WERE REVEALED AND I SURRENDERED TO THE CALL WITHIN, I WAS ABLE TO LET GO OF THE NEED FOR ANOTHER'S LOVE TO FEEL HAPPY ....**

Just as I thought my "love" could save others, I thought a woman's love could make me safe and happy.

Isn't that what TV and movies teach us?

My forsaken child would have me jump from one relationship to another looking to feel Loved, Safe, Validated, Seen, and Happy.

When the relationship would start going sideways or there were ever arguments, it would trigger all of my wounds from childhood.

It must all be my fault so I would beat myself up.

I would immediately start trying to make her happy so the fear of abandonment would subside and the fear of her going away would leave.

I would grab on So tightly that I would suffocate her and us.

When the physical touch or intimacy would be taken away, my anxiety, fears, and abandonments would kick into high gear. So I would mask that by staying busy as a workaholic and overachiever.

Over and over, I would make excuses to not go home so I didn't have to feel the rejection by my spouse.

Going home became a sad and painful event, especially when there was no touch.

I would do anything to avoid rejection and conflict because it would just destroy me inside.

To have met one's true self is the greatest gift you will ever receive.

To surrender to your purpose and bring your essence to the world is the greatest gift you can contribute to humanity

Today, I will turn inward to feel safe, happy, and loved.

I HAVE HEALED MYSELF (MOSTLY) FROM THE INSIDE OUT BY CONNECTING WITH THE DIVINITY WITHIN ME ....

My divine light was lying dormant, waiting for me to wake up and activate ME (my essence) and my truth!

I could not handle nor hear the divine downloads I receive today until I surrendered completely and began the Alchemical change required to transmute myself into The Divine Being I am.

My surrender, acceptance, letting go, and trusting were the keys that unlocked the door to a 180-degree change in everything!

I made choices to change everything in my life in order to clear the way for this calling to become clearer and clearer.

I accepted the call without questioning it.

Undeniable alignments and synchronicities began happening daily. Relationships faded and new healthier ones took their place.

People began showing up with gifts to help my progression.

My thought process began changing and I saw life with crystal clarity.

I knew the choices I was making would bless everyone in my life in ways I knew they were incapable of seeing at the time.

I realized everyone in my life would be blessed even though they were blind to see how.

Feeling the divinity within my blood was an energetic feeling I had not known.

I felt a Love I had never known and it wasn't coming from a woman. It was originating in ME.

What I 'want' is my lower frequency trying to draw me away from my path.

Tapping into my 'higher self' relieves me of the burden of wanting anything that holds me back from ascending and evolving.

Today, the Divine Being I am is awake and willing to do all the Creator lays at my feet.

TRADED IN MY PHD (PROGRAMMED HUMAN DEVELOPMENT) FOR MY SBA (SPIRITUAL BEING ALIGNMENT) ....

Being able to look at myself as the problem, I was able to see how "I had allowed life and people" to warp and control my thoughts and decisions.

I began the business of rewiring myself based on the new life experiences I was creating.

I began being an information gatherer, and my classroom was my heart, and my soul and spirit were my guides. All information is now brought into my chest for discernment as to whether it is my truth, not my truth, or needs experience behind it before making that decision. Once I truly feel the answer within, I can send the message to my brain, creating the heart/brain connection.

I do my best not to repeat what I hear before I do this process, or I'm just a parrot repeating someone else's perception of truth.

I don't go to a workshop and tell everyone what I "just learned." I have not learned anything.... I've just heard one person's or group's belief/perception.

I DO NOT HAVE WISDOM WITHOUT EXPERIENCE!

If I don't have the experience, I'm not capable of sharing anything as I would just be making shit up to sound Cool or Smart.

Saying "I don't have experience with that " is honoring my truth and being authentic.

As my soul becomes more aligned and becomes more one with the Divine Creator, I feel more personally empowered to speak my truth without caring how it's received.

I know I am speaking clearly as I have surrendered to His/Her will for me.

Today my soul truth is being revealed more and more, and I can't wait to see what is next.

Willingness to Drill Deep into Each Wound and Then Fearlessly Drill Deeper Still ....

The deeper I go, the more I grow!

The deeper my roots, the higher I can ascend.

When we choose our addictions and suffering over our healing, we push away people and opportunities sent to us by our Higher Self.

Our radiant and vibrational frequencies originate from a place of self-loathing, shame, guilt, and unworthiness.

The past is the past, and no matter how terrible and difficult it was, you have a choice today to stop feeding it your power and energy.

Get busy living or get busy dying. Doing the necessary healing work or continuing to suffer is a choice ....

Will you love yourself enough today to battle the beasts within that bind you to this illusion created by fear?

Nothing matters ... all you leave with is what you came with, so let it go and choose love over fear.

You're worth it, and the world heals when you heal.

Every time I want a new level of consciousness, I have to be willing to dive deeper and deeper into my wounds and blocks.

Every time I did this, it was like my being would be lifted a bit higher, giving me access to information and downloads I was open to receiving.

It still works like this today.

When I transmuted the wounds and pulled my power back, my ability to open up grew exponentially.

Today I don't fight or struggle with the deeper dives because I know what lies around the corner every time; I'm willing to do so.

I have to descend the light into the dark in order to raise the dark higher into the light.

The deeper the descension, the higher the ascension!

Today, I will go deeper than I ever have because I'm worth it! No More Holding the World Hostage ....

The World Was Held Hostage to My Excessive Demands...

When they weren't met, I stood in my crib crying and banging my rattle on the side, begging for someone to feel sorry for me!

No more feeling like I'm owed something (victim).

No more expectations of others and/or situations.

No more "The World According to Ocean".

I held the world hostage to the demands, expectations, and desires I thought I was owed.

I would especially hold women hostage to my inner demands and desires.

Because of my childhood experiences, I felt like life should come easy to me.

Life was never fair, and I always set my expectations Higher than anyone or any situation could ever live up to.

I set myself up to be let down over and over again. It was my fault!

No one could live up to what I thought I was supposed to receive.

Nothing I received ever filled the holes inside me, so I always felt like I should have more.

I no longer have expectations and I release attachments of how people should behave and what results should be.

I've let go of old beliefs that money, possessions, and women could make me happy.

Less on the outside means More on the Inside!

I bring the best me to the situation, do my part with Love for my fellow man and woman, and leave the results to the Creator.

"The lower my expectations, the higher my level of happiness!"

Today, the world and people owe me nothing and I owe the world a life lived in service to all.

WHAT'S MY PART? BECAUSE YOUR PART IS NONE OF MY BUSINESS! ....

Releasing the victim within took many deep hard looks into the mirror.

I have a part in everything in my life, and I'm the common denominator!

I wanted to blame others and life for my problems.

I always had an excuse for my problems and what I deemed as failures.

I would blame others for my problems and become attached to the resentments and hate I held inside as suffering was my addiction.

I have a choice in every situation and who I keep in my life.

If something or someone is not serving my highest and best good, I remove them or it with love.

I love everyone as my brothers and sisters, but most need to be loved from a distance as I do not resonate or vibrate with them.

I chose my part with regard to my old story.

I may not have been able to control what took place when I was a child, but I'm damn sure responsible for the power/energy I give away.

If I choose not to do the necessary work to regain the power I was born with, I'm choosing to stay in the story and allow resentment and hate to be my masters.

My old story subconsciously controlled my thoughts and actions.

I didn't understand why I was stuck and repeating choices that kept putting me back in the same unhealthy situations and relationships.

It had to be Her fault, right?

Wrong, she was who she was when I met her ... I wasn't healthy enough to say no when I saw the red flags out of fear of rejection and not being loved.

My wounding set my relationships on a path that was doomed.

Looking at 'Your' part in the story was always a deflection of energy that should be directed at ME.

> Today, I will only look at my part and release
> the resentments that became my master!

EMBRACE OTHER'S HUMANNESS ....

I used to sit around and judge others all the time.

It was much easier to point out other people's flaws (according to my perception) than look at my own.

Almost every time I did this, I was judging them for something I didn't like about myself. I tore people apart in order to build myself up.

Whenever I would point one finger at you, I had three pointing back at me. I look back at what a complete hypocrite I was.

I had to meet people where they were in life as I have never walked One Step in anyone else's shoes.

Compassion and non-judgment towards others came only after I was able to love and have compassion for myself.

Until that point, I loved and gave compassion with price tags.

There had to be something in it for me, and I would set expectations before being compassionate to your needs or actions I didn't approve of.

Understanding we all have walked different paths with different life experiences helped me open my heart to all.

Each time someone finds love within themselves, love grows in the collective whole.

I love ME, so love just exist.

Love is the Force that will heal the world.

The more I love ME,
The deeper love exists in You.

Today, I accept others for who they are and their journey to love is none of my business!

The Mother's call cries to my soul
Beckoning me to forget All I know.
She is here to help hold my pain
Telling me I am not the one to blame.
Ripping open wounds from the past
To show others, the pain won't last.
She kept me alive for a divine reason
Now it is time to embrace that season.
A season and time to help show others
We are connected, sisters and brothers.
When your call comes, don't shy away
Answer and surrender to it today.
The time has come to stand together,
For we are all Divinely Tethered.

Ocean Eagle

WORLDLY DOMESTICATION SERVED ITS PURPOSE ....

Living from the false truth which was domestically pro-grammed kept me in emotional and spiritual Hell and on "life support." I never understood why life was such a damn struggle and fight all the time.

I was used to homes and people going away, so it didn't kill me when this happened. It was my programmed expectation for everything to fall apart without notice.

Besides, I had my good buddy alcohol around until I was 30 to numb the pain and survived the next 20 years with other forms of addiction. My false ego mask kept me trudging through life.

Work, golf, exercise, family, and ad nauseum became my drugs of choice. Anything to escape feeling and keep building the mask I hid behind.

I have let go of all domestication and I live a life led by the Spirit. This required letting go of everything my mind thought it knew.

From the center of my heart, I ask myself if an opportunity or person aligns with my divine truth and purpose, my essence! If not, I do not sacrifice my self-worth by going against myself. I don't please people and I don't owe anyone anything.

I no longer make choices based on money as I have let go of that attachment as well.

My will has been turned over to the Creator and I have never felt so loved and supported.

I'm finally living the heart-centered life I never knew I wanted. S.A.L.T. helps me clean my lenses daily in order to see beyond the veil.

Today, false domestication no longer serves me so
I release the grip I allowed it to have over ME.

IF IT DOESN'T SERVE ME, IT DOESN'T DESERVE ME.......

I'll start by saying AMEN!!!!!!!

I think I could write an entire book on this, and I just might if it calls to me.

Today, I allow myself to be completely selfish when it comes to Honoring and Validating ME!

How long did I allow people and situations to stick around based on Fear and what others expected and thought of me?

Other's expectations are none of my business, and I now understand most people are not awake, so why would I ever have listened to them anyway?

It was because I felt like I owed the world something and that it owed me something.

How many jobs did I stay in?

How often did I say yes when I truly wanted to say was ... Hell No!

I owe it to myself to align my will with the truth within my chest.

The truth of a divinely given essence by my Creator designed just for ME.

When I show up in an authentic and vulnerable way, I attract those who are supposed to be in my life and those who are not just fall away without effort.

I deserve to be happy, loved, and supported.

I don't look for Love in people or worldly possessions today.

I serve ME as it aligns to my Creator and my Creator, in turn, blesses me beyond anything I could ever put on a dream board so I don't have one!

I have everything I need within.

Today, I honor and love Me by saying NO!

I Can See Clearly Now, and All External Obsessions Continue to Lose their Flavor ....

Today, I am not obsessed with anything or anyone. My obsession is the desire to help this planet and its inhabitants Evolve.

I used to play golf all the time and I used to exercise obsessively.

Since my awakening and complete surrender to my calling, I have played golf once in 42 months and could care less if I ever play again.

I used to be an exceptionally good golfer who had to practice daily and play 3-4 times a week or I was restless, irritable, and discontent.

Everyone suffered when I didn't get to play or practice.

Likewise with exercising, if I missed a workout I was so anxious and felt like years of workouts would disappear overnight.

If I knew I was going out of town or had to miss a day or two, I was super upset and would work out twice a day before and after to "make up" the lost days.

Today I just miss those days and I don't feel like I'm going to lose everything I had worked for physically.

My diet was not the best for years and I know I paid the price for these choices. Food is such a tricky obsession for those in its grips.

I trained my body to see food as fuel and only eat when my body tells me to.

We are programmed to eat 3 meals a day but we don't always need it.

I allow life to flow and I eat mindfully most of the time to honor the temple that is my body.

This attitude works for everything in my life now ... just flow like water and move in the directions laid at my feet every day.

Today, I release my obsessions and validate and honor myself by doing so!

I Feel Happy and Whole When I am Serving Others ....

I'm always happy inside, no matter what life throws at me today.

Serving the Creator's desire for me makes my heart feel pure joy on top of the happiness.

Seeing others gain hope and inspiration from anything I do excites my soul and inspires me to keep going.

Watching others conquer the demon that is their Old Story and awaken to their Truth and Divine Purpose is a such a gift

Knowing they have truly Surrendered and Accepted the Great Mystery of the Unknown within brings me to tears.

When I have tough moments of self-doubt and life is throwing growth opportunities my way, serving others always pulls me out of feeling sorry for myself or complaining.

My problems go away when I am helping another get through their difficulties and trials.

The best medicine for troubling times
is to be of service to other humans.

When I am doing the job for this planet and its inhabitants that I'm meant to do, I have endless energy and rarely get tired. To be there when the light bulb gets turned on or have someone send me a message letting me know they get it now, is a blessing all should experience. It's the best fuel to stay on the healing path.

I know what it means to let go of everything and what gifts and blessings it will bring to a person, their family, and this planet.

Won't you love yourself enough to let go of the old story?

Today, My Happiness Truly Comes from Service to Others!

SERVING THE DIVINE MOTHER'S CALL IS LIKE TASTING NECTAR DRIPPING FROM HER FINGERTIPS AND I CAN'T GET ENOUGH ....

It truly feels like this to me today.

I can imagine the Divine Mother's fingers reaching down from the sky and the Nectar of wisdom, grace, compassion, and love are dripping from them.

My Crown Chakra is wide open and there is now a clear path into my Heart and Soul for that nectar to drip into as it feeds and nourishes ME.

Once within me, I can expand my heart and the capacity to Love and give Compassion to all grows endlessly.

I had to clear that path before
I could receive this gift.

That means I had to do the ugly, dark work hardly anyone is willing to do. I had to look at buried things I had hidden away and compartmentalized in my mind.

No wonder few will surrender to a journey such as this!

It's not for the faint of heart but for those who have received The Gifts of Desperation, a journey to the center of the soul you won't want to miss!

My expansion happens daily, and I'm excited to wake up every day!

Today, I choose to remain open to the Divine Mother's flow of the sweet nectar of love and wisdom!

I Finally See ME, and I am Beautifull ....

I am the Divine Truth I was always seeking.

I was sent here with Everything I needed to be Whole, Safe, Loved, and Happy.

It is No Longer the world's job to satisfy my worldly desires and demands as I have let them all go. I am no longer a slave to the things and the people I thought I needed to make me whole.

That is between my Creator and Me ....

What I thought I wanted, who I thought I was, and who I thought I should be is all gone now.

I am a Beautiful Being of Light designed and kept alive to activate the souls of those ready to be awakened to their purpose. Serving others tethers me to happiness and joy.

I hope to touch as many souls as possible with the message being delivered through me from the Creator so we may all evolve into a higher state of consciousness.

I feel once enough of us have changed our vibrational frequency, and the world will begin to finally heal.

The beauty I saw in you that I longed for I now see in me.

I look in the mirror of life, and I see beauty without the world's validation. One day at a time, I continue to evolve into the best version of ME and trust the guidance of my higher self.

Beauty is truly within!!!!

> Today, I am beautiful just as I am!

NOTHING ON THE EXTERNAL CAN TOUCH ME NOW AS DIVINITY DWELLS IN MY HEART AND SOUL ....

I'm not afraid to die now.

I'm not afraid of You now.

I'm not afraid to fail now.

I'm not afraid of being hurt today.

I'm not afraid to be by myself today.

I'm not afraid to take risks today.

I'm not afraid to go against societal programming.

I'm not afraid of money today.

Divinity swims in my blood, and my DNA/Cells have been activated.

The fear that kept me alive no longer has a place in my life.

Deep inside, I know nothing in this earthly existence can touch me.

It doesn't mean my old story can't be triggered. It means that I know how to quickly realize, recognize, and have a reckoning with the trigger on the spot and move on instead of getting stuck in the emotion brought up.

I no longer have to hold the world hostage to my trigger and past.

Likewise, I can see and be discerning about people stuck in the old story and dreams. When I recognize red flags, I pause and sit in the observer's seat. I no longer have a false ego telling me I can love them enough to heal them or mold them into what I want them to be. It's none of my business!

I keep all at a very healthy distance if it appears they are not open to a new way of feeling and living. Not my way, just an opening and desire to be willing to turn inward for their answers.

Healthy boundaries are paramount to being a healthy Ocean Eagle!

We are all divine beings of light; we just have to remember who we truly are!

Today, I choose to trust the Creator's will, not my false ego's program!

I FEEL THIS EXISTENCE IS LESS THAN A SNAP OF MY FINGERS IN TIME AND SPACE ....

I used to worry and stress over the smallest things.

If a bomb went off and all of creation was going to be vaporized in 5 minutes, would anything I was stressing about really matter?

Death is the greatest teacher we have on earth, I believe.

Just watch what happens when someone knows their life will end soon.

Would you spend time in the house or car you are so deeply attached to?

Would that collection of worldly items be so treasured?

Would those bank accounts be so important?

Would having a certain amount of money at retirement be so Valued?

I don't believe we take any of the pain from this life to the other side either.

The only thing I'm taking with me is what I came with, my essence (ME).

I'm either taking a soul home that evolved or didn't evolve the way it was meant to during this incarnation.

If I did the evolving I was supposed to do, I get to move on to a higher level of consciousness in the next incarnation.

I have no proof of that; it's just my inner knowing.

What and who can you let go of today to support you, who you are meant to be?

Life is so short! Why not go all in and surrender to the life you were meant to live?

To me, you have nothing to lose and everything to gain!

Today, I choose LIFE and to live like I'm dying tomorrow!!

I AM MY HIGHEST AND BEST SELF AND LOVED FROM ABOVE! ....

Earth feeds my being
Fire ignites my soul
Water gently flows within
Wind directs my wings

My Divine Mother and Father direct all I do today.

I finally have the relationship with my parents I always dreamed of.

My parents, who truly made ME, showed me that I am doing the work I was sent here to do every day.

They are proud of me.
They show up for me.
They encourage me.
They are patient with me.
They hold me tightly.
They inspire me.
They strengthen me.
They share wisdom with me.
They love me.

Alignments, not accidents or coincidences, happen throughout my day and I know it is their guiding grace working in my life as a beacon.

Synchronicities that could never happen, happen all the time.

Numerology is off the charts and the odds of them happening the way they do are astronomical.

Of course they are astronomical, that's where my home is and where I long to return!

Today I will show up as my highest and best self,
giving the love I am receiving to others freely!

I Love taking Day Breaks in my Head ....

When I need a break from the world or feel anxious and I cannot get to nature, I go there in my mind.

I take deep breaths in a quiet place until I can get out of the frontal lobe of my brain and drop into my chest.

The breath takes me home whenever I need to go there.

The place in my heart and right below it where I feel my divine light and soul's essence.

It's my classroom where I am both teacher and student.

Once there, all unnecessary anxiety leaves as I am reminded of what this is all about.

Life is not about whatever it is I feel is so important at that moment.

I should never willingly give my problems my energy or personal power. It's my fault when I do, so it is up to me to fix it internally and not with outside distractions or addictions.

When I meditate I am able to step out of the dream and into conscious awareness.

I can be grounded no matter what is going on the outside.

I practice being present and aware 24/7. Even in a crowded situation, I can stay calm and peaceful by just closing my eyes, building an energetic bubble around me and dwelling in the nothingness of the stillness within.

Chaos is no longer my master!

Today, I choose meditative inner peace
over anxiety and stress!

I WAS CONDITIONED BY THE MEANINGS I ATTACHED TO WORDS ....

When I changed the meanings I assigned to words, it removed the power they had over me.

I constantly suggest to people that they remove words that do not serve their higher self.

We are programmed to rely on the meanings of words society feeds us from birth. That's why it's called "spelling," as it actually casts 'spells' over you.

Words like Hard, Difficult, Want, Hope, and Maybe.

The work I did in the years leading up to my awakening was Necessary in order to evolve into who I am today.

If I kept saying things were hard and difficult, guess what? They were hard and difficult, and I did not want to do them.

Yoda told Luke Skywalker, "Do or Do Not, There is No Try!".

I no longer hope to do things or go places ... I do them and go there!

I'm definite with my choices, and I say yes or no ... there is No Maybe.

I may need time to let it resonate with me, but that is not the same as Maybe.

I no longer say I want things as I live in S.A.L.T.

Surrender, Accept, Let Go, and Trust.

I also change my mind when I need to.

Saying yes to something does not mean I have to stick with it if I find out it does not align with my truth.

That is not the same as not doing something I have committed to because something better came along.

Having Integrity builds my self-esteem.

Toda,y I build the world on the outside by choosing words that make them the reality and validate ME!

My Brain and Heart are My Spiritual Teepee ....

As I stoke the fires of truth in my heart and soul, the messages are carried up like smoke billowing up to the top of a teepee, feeding my brain with love, inspiration, compassion, guidance, discernment, and joy.

Sometimes when I drop into my heart, I imagine sitting in the middle of a Native American teepee with a large fire in the middle.

As I commune within myself in the center of the teepee, I imagine the information needing discernment swirling around in the flames.

When I receive my answer, I watch the message rise through the ashes and through the top of the teepee where my brain receives the instructions on how to proceed in the world.

The more I know my soul and validate its truth, the more the fire within me grows.

It's an unstoppable force, and I am not trying to harness it.

Once wounds are revealed and healed, they become fuel to stoke the inner flame of our Divine Purpose as we are now fully empowered and no longer powerless ....

> Today, I choose to stoke the fire in my inner teepee and listen for my truth as it rises through the ashes of all that is false!

BOOKS INSPIRE ME; THEY DON'T TEACH ME.

I gather the information I resonate with from books I read and take it to the classroom in my chest, where my truth lies.

My heart and soul are my information decipherers.

My heart and soul let me know what is true and false for ME! I become the teacher at the chalkboard and the student observing.

It may be true for you and not for me, and that is Okay!

Your truth is none of my business, and I don't waste my time trying to get people to see things my way.

That's why it's called "My Truth" and not "Our Truth."

As with everything and Everyone in life, it's all just information and energy needing discernment so we can grow. When I read a book I simply retain the parts that might be right for me.

If I start sharing something I read before I gain my own wisdom behind it, I'm sharing the perception of the person who wrote the book and I'm just a parrot.

I've spoken with many who go to "Guru's or Master's" weekend retreats or workshops and return trying to guide others with the new information they received. For me, until I have an awareness of the parts that were meant for me and apply them to my own life, I have nothing to share with others.

It's only authentically mine once I
gain wisdom through experience.

It's not wisdom until I have the experience, and then all I have is my wisdom. I share it in hopes it attracts those it may resonate with and inspire them to search within themselves. We were born as the answer. Information and wisdom unlock the doors to deeper soul retrieval and truth.

Today, I allow information to come in but it's
not my wisdom prior to investigation!

Awoken Beings Activate and Inspire Others to Go Deeper Within ....

Just as I feel I am a soul activator, so are others to me.

It does not mean I make them my Guru or Master.

It means I respect the way they guide and the integrity they live by.

I'm willing to look at their offerings and become Inspired to fearlessly surrender to a calling as they have.

My message and its delivery may be different or similar but the Passion and Desire to serve the world are aligned.

The call to awake is for everyone to access.

But I feel some have been called to help activate those who are open and willing to receive.

It's a responsibility I do not take lightly and I feel the planets and humanity's existence depend on it.

I believe that once enough have woken up and changed their vibration and consciousness, the world will begin to come together in global Unity. It will take a global exercise of letting go of an old paradigm whose time has run its course.

Do I have scientific evidence? Nope!

Can I show you where it is written in an ancient text? Nope!

Can I take you to an ancient site where it's written in hieroglyphics? Nope!

Let's just call it Divine Intuition within my soul written in my DNA. When my awakening happened on May 4, 2019, I was blessed with an inner knowing of my purpose for being here .... My Essence. The immediate feeling of love for all humans and the planet is a gift I wish for all to experience.

Today, I am open to allowing others to Inspire and Activate me in order to Go Deeper and Further!

THERE IS A DEPTH TO ME THAT IS UNIQUE....

I'm deep in my own way.

Just because others have woken up does not mean we are the same.

I believe I have a calling and purpose designed specifically for me.

I do not think I am special or better than another being. Those who vibrate at similar frequencies will gather as they tap into that frequency on a higher level.

They will gravitate toward one another effortlessly.

The depth of my soul is no deeper than anyone else's, but I feel it is specifically designed for me and I'm being guided to those I must serve and help on their journey home.

I don't feel that everyone has the same blueprint or calling.

I feel everyone has a specific essence the Creator gave to them.

Having known mine, I can die in peace now knowing I'm walking in and sharing the Creator's love with all.

I would have been very disappointed had I died and then found out I just lived this earthly programmed life without tasting this!

I wouldn't trade the first 50 years of my life (minus my children) for the last 42 months any day.

I am eternally grateful for everything that happened in those 50 years as they were the building blocks and wounding

I so desperately needed .... The Gifts of Desperation gut me to my knees and gratitude washed away my pain!

Today, I swim in the depths of my soul
and rejoice in knowing my truth.

My Gratitude Changed
my Attitude ....

A Victim No More I walk this world with my head held high.

I've seen the most amazing cloud designs and sacred geometry in the sky because I'm no longer looking at the tops of my shoes.

Once I became Grateful for everything that happened in my life, I no longer regretted or hated my past.

I no longer Was my past!

On the evening of my awakening, I looked deeply into my eyes in the mirror and sobbed as I finally saw me, loved me, and felt such deep Compassion for ME ... I made It. All I suffered was no longer in vain.

Loving who I am today means I don't regret anything or anyone from my past because if I changed one thing, it would have altered my course, and I may have never arrived at this point.

I am grateful for all ... No better or bad judgments about my story, just unconditional gratitude!

The pain and suffering I went through molded me into the man I love today.

Being grateful also allowed me to let go of the wounds and people of my past I was unwilling to forgive.

When I became grateful for everything and everyone in my past, it was as if I had immediate compassion for them.

I want to thank every human being along my path back home to ME. Thanks to you, I now authentically embody love and compassion for others as I now possess it for myself.

Today I am grateful for everything that made ME!

Living in Fantasy Vs. Reality ....

Trying to love from the wounded heart was a repeated effort in futility. Like the alcoholic, who thinks after a brief period of time they can drink like "normal" drinkers, I kept forgetting how bad my relationships turned out, so I kept going back to the well.

Again, the "Common Denominator" in all of my failed relationships was Me!

Once I started pointing the finger at myself instead of them, I slowly saw my part.

I was no longer looking at them as the problem.

I picked them! Even though they had their part, I was the one who tried to Love before I ever loved myself.

I wanted their love to fix me and fill the hole within me they never could.

Once again, as with everything, I turn inward and see with crystal vision because nothing ever stuck or lasted.

When the made-up fantasy wore off, I was always slapped with the reality of what I had gotten myself into.

My default programming from childhood was to duck and run from my problems.

My wounded child always hated the thought of relationships not working out because it must be my fault!

Nothing worse than Reality hitting you in the forehead when you have committed to someone and realizing you just made a huge mistake.

Especially when there are children involved.

For me, staying in a relationship, I know I should not be in poison everyone involved.

Today, there are no mistakes, just opportunities to go deeper.

Not letting go out of fear or shame leads to fear, anxiety, and resentment later.

> Today I live in the reality of love and compassion for myself, and I'm enjoying getting to know ME!

I DON'T KNOW WHAT I THOUGHT I KNEW ....

Unknowing all I thought I knew has been part of my alchemical process to purge a false belief system that no longer served me.

I am grateful for the belief system as it kept me alive through many devastating times in my life.

Everything I believed in and thought was true was based on the false agreements and deals I made with life-based on unhealed wounding from events and people in my life.

Wounding both out of my control and self-inflicted.

Until I began to see through the mask I had created to stay alive and safe, I stayed stuck and unable to see outside the world I created to keep me protected.

I overlaid my inability to trust anyone on all unsuspecting victims in my path.

Looking outside, the story was scary and unsafe.

I was driven and directed by the fear of the unknown and what society said was the truth.

Once I woke up, I immediately decided to surrender to the Creator's will and abandon myself!

When I realized we are all one consciousness, it was not a difficult decision to make.

I put my life in the loving hands of the Divine Source that created me.

Today I live in the "nothingness of the unknown stillness" within.

The magic of "The Great Mystery".

I'm finally in the back seat and no longer driving the bus.

It's about forgetting everything I used in the past to survive to make room for a brand-new way of Living!

One of my sticky notes on my refrigerator says, "I Know Nothing", which is about starting over from nothing as I gather information and gain brand new wisdom.

> Today, I'm grateful for my old belief
> system, but I now let it go!

I can blow like the Wind
I can illuminate as the Sun
I can flow as the Ocean
I can be steady as Stone
I can fly high as the Stars
I can be tender as the Moon
I can be all-encompassing
I am timeless as the universe
Divinity lies within my soul
Everything is ME, and this I Know!

~ Ocean

Pachamama Feeds and Nourishes My Vessel So My Spirit May Shine Divine Light from Above Like a Beacon of Hope for the World ....

In the Andean and Inca traditions, Pachamama is a fertility Goddess who watches over the earth's planting and harvest.

We must walk softly on Her and be mindful of how we treat the one who feeds and nourishes All.

I am more mindful of the footprint I leave anywhere I go and where I live.

When I think about the amount of trash just one NFL football game that generates, it sickens my heart.

When I think about all of the events around the world that generate trash that we put back into the soil that feeds us, it's difficult to imagine.

I want to treat Mother Earth with the same love and respect I give to my body.

If I am willing to treat the earth poorly, I'm probably treating myself poorly.

We all die and go back into Pachamama, as does everything in the world.

Even furniture, at some point, goes back into the earth.

We are all one as we are all fed and nourished by the same Earth and we all die back to her.

She turns everything back into nutrients that we later consume to grow and flourish.

Developing a healthy attitude and respect for Her means we are respecting all who reside here.

Today, I will mindfully care for Mother Earth and be grateful for her life-sustaining nourishment!

THE SUN WAKES AND STIRS ME EVERY DAY!

Every morning is a grand rising and rebirth for the planet and each of us.

As the sun comes up over the horizon in the morning, I am in humble gratitude for its love and life-enriching rays.

It reminds me of the rebirthing process I always need to experience if I want to grow.

Much like an infant coming through its mother's womb, rebirthing parts of me can be a struggle and painful.

Who in their right mind wants to do anything that feels like this?

That is where The Gifts of Desperation comes in for me.

Normally I have to be in a lot of pain and suffering before I begin the work necessary to change.

Much like the serpents I have tattooed on my forearm, I have to shed the old parts of me that no longer serve me.

To be reborn, I must die as the sun sets and disappears nightly.

Our inhale and exhale is a constant practice
in breathing in life and exhaling death...
everything no longer serving our body.

I try to think of what part of me needs to die today so that when the sun comes back up in the morning, that part of me can be rebirthed with a new awareness that is aligned with the Creator's will.

An example we all struggle with is the judgment of others. This process will continue forever for me as I will never be a perfected being, so I am thankful for the daily nudge from Father Sun to keep looking at myself in order to see what needs to die in order to be reborn.

Today, I will embrace every opportunity to be born anew!

I Will Show My Awakening to the World to Inspire Others to Seek Theirs ....

Time to shine my light ... The divinely placed Inca Seed is centered in the seat of my soul.

For me, once I had shown ME (my essence) and my purpose, there was no way to deny it as it ignited a fire and passion within me I had never experienced.

It felt like I had been lying dormant and just existing, waiting for this "AHA!" moment.

The moment when everything in you vibrates at a frequency that touches the tips of every nerve ending in your body!

Trying to deny this would be like not eating food or drinking water.

I would be starting to feel it again, so I chose to go All In with complete abandon to the Creator's will.

In May 2019, I went home after my awakening at the gathering of the Shamans, and I changed one thing ... everything!

I created a Facebook page to connect with this new world and show the world everything about me.

A therapist would cringe at the thought of what I have done, as I have shared most of my demons and past with the world openly.

We are programmed to keep it secret and behind doors, as others will judge us.

For Me, knowing who I am, means I don't care about what anyone thinks of me anymore.

I'm free to be ME!

I walk my awakening daily, and I pray to inspire others to abandon themselves to their inner work and see if they can ignite their inner flame of truth!

Today, I will freely share my awakening and truth with anyone ready to receive the gifts I have to share.

WE ARE ALL ALCHEMISTS ....

As the Alchemist of old, I am constantly working on myself through the various steps of alchemy.

When I researched alchemy, it became evident to me that alchemy was already working on me before I began the process.

Alchemists of old believed in order to purify metals and turn them into gold, they must first purify themselves in order to gain the power to complete the process.

They would have a separate space for meditation and focus on certain drawings and images (mandalas) in order to transform themselves.

The first step is calcination, and one must burn off all attachments to all material things and, for me, any and all attachments to anyone.

Letting go of all attachments was something I'd already been working on, so the process had already begun.

As I looked deeper into my past, I could see that all 7 steps had been repeating themselves throughout my life.

Getting sober over 23 years ago was another step 1 as I let go of the attachment to alcohol.

Releasing attachments to people has been a huge part of this process as I honor ME by letting go of relationships not serving ME.

Calcination—Controlled burn by deliberate surrender
Dissolution—Release of emotions controlling and distorting
   our truth
Separation—Letting go of self-inflicted restraints and beliefs

Conjunction—Union of feminine and masculine within oneself

Fermentation—Flooding our mind with profound images/ meditation

Distillation—Introspection to raise our psyche to its highest and best

Coagulation—Owning the universal gold and power of the universe. The force that overcomes and penetrates every subtle and solid thing!

> Today, I surrender to the process of Alchemy in order to have the mysteries of all things revealed!

I will Help Bring Balance to the Masculine and Feminine Energies That Have Spiraled Out of Control ....

To me, this is the most important work on the planet!

The old paradigm of this Patriarchal system is falling apart, and its time is coming to an end.

Those still stuck in this are grasping for straws and desperately trying to hold onto their grip on power, money, and humans.

Likewise, the old religious powers are crumbling as humans are waking up and seeing how religions rule by manipulation, fear, shame, and control. No human has the right to tell another human what to do or how to live their life.

So, many throw stones from glass houses as they deflect their own lack of self-esteem and shame by pointing out what they judge as others' shortcomings. My father and my childhood in West Texas hardwired me to believe showing my feelings and emotions was weak. My father modeled the unhealthiest version of masculinity to me. He always had a bigger and better story and used fear, anger, and physical abuse to control his environment.

He treated women as objects to use as he wished.

Because of men with this hardwired belief system, women have had to go deep into masculinity in order to make up for the lack of healthy masculine energy from men and to protect themselves. When a woman feels the energy of a healthy 'Masculine', it must feel extraneous. But once the guard comes down and allows that energy to penetrate deeply, it begins the healing process. Women understand how to show emotions with other women but don't trust that men can hold it without the man wanting to fix the woman.

Learning how to hold a healthy, safe space for a woman has been Soul healing for ME.

Today, I will constantly be aware of both
the Feminine and Masculine Within!

I AM CONNECTED TO ALL THROUGH THE VIBRATIONS OF ENERGY, MATTER, AND SOUND! THE RESONATION OF THE UNIVERSAL FREQUENCY MATRIX IS MY GUIDE AND ARRANGES THE DETAILS OF MY LIFE BY HARMONIZING AND BALANCING MY INNER-CHI!

The Will and The Womb
Yin and Yang
Spirit and Matter
Light and Dark
Sound and Stillness
Hot and Cold

Heavy and Light
Love and Hate
Good and Bad
Evil and Kindness
Above and Below
Strong and Weak

There is no separation and no difference, just connected and balanced order.

Today I will ground myself by practicing meditation, spending time in nature and sitting in the awareness of all I am and all that is!

I Don't Think in Absolutes Anymore ....

It does not serve me to speak of myself or anyone else in absolutes. The old me would look at the man I am today and say, "I can't become that or do that".

I didn't even know I wanted this life.

Likewise, it's not my job to tell others what they can and cannot become or do.

Someone told me, "You know you can't heal anyone, right?"

I think people can do what they believe they can do and receive what they need based on the energy and power they give it.

I don't know if I'm healing someone, they are healing themselves, or we are doing it together. It's none of my business!

To me, it's based on the level of faith each one has.

I don't call myself a healer of others but I believe I am healing myself.

I know I have affected others along their path to go deeper within.

I've laid hands on people with migraines who were out dancing with our group shortly afterward.

Did I heal her?

All I know is that her migraine went away after I placed my hands on her head as I sent all the love I could through them to help her.

She believed I helped her but it was more about the self-healing she manifested through her own energy.

If I say things as absolute truth, then it is the end of that thought or belief. Living in the flow of abundant energy from the inside out,

I remain open to change and new ideas.

This is why I don't have a dream board, or as I call them, a Suffering Board. I just flow with the Creator's energy and guidance.

It's way more fun that way as I am always amazed and surprised.

> Today, I will leave the channel of Love from the Creator wide open to the amazement that awaits ME!

TEACHERS TELL YOU HOW TO SOLVE A PROBLEM WHILE GUIDES HELP YOU FIND THE SOLUTIOM BY ARRIVING AT THE ANSWER YOURSELF ....

In my opinion, the best guides ask questions to the answers you are seeking.

When I find the answer within, it becomes my wisdom and not something I read in a textbook.

I pay attention to those who have what I want and investigate how they became who they are.

I don't model them precisely as I am not them. I take the guidance from their actions that I resonate with and apply them to my life to see if they work for me.

To me, the only masters on earth are children and nature.

The children of the world remind me how to love, laugh, forgive, play, be silly, be creative, serve others, and live with innocents.

When I just sit and watch children, they are in their own world and don't care what anyone around them thinks ... they know who they are!

Interesting that that has been the biggest part of my transformation, just playing like a child again and not caring what others think.

I spend a lot of time in nature walking on beaches by the ocean, strolling through a trail in the trees, listening to the birds sing, sitting on top of granite stones, meditating by the moving water of a river, hanging out in a cave, and being still on top of a mountain.

I receive information, downloads and inspiration every time!

Mother Nature reminds me how connected I am to her and everything as she is the source of life-giving nutrients and oxygen to all living things.

Today, I will become both teacher and student
as I bring the information I receive from
my Guides to my heart's classroom!

ISN'T ALL THAT WE THOUGHT
WE KNEW CONSTANTLY
BEING DISPROVED?......

Why would we limit ourselves to thinking scientists and archeologists have it all figured out?

Isn't just about everything we thought they knew being disproved? They have no idea how the human brain works and no real idea how old the pyramids are in Egypt.

We are constantly finding ruins of lost cities hidden within the ocean waters. I've heard we may have only uncovered about 5-10% of what is really buried in the sands of Egypt.

I've been in the mountains in Peru and seen countless Inca terrace walls covered by forest still.

What secrets are the jungles of Mesoamerica and Brazil hiding?

We just have no idea, and we will not know in this incarnation.

I hope we focus on understanding there was ancient wisdom on the planet thousands and thousands of years ago that was deeper and more intelligent than we are today.

I don't need to know the how and why of ancient times or structures.

I feel in my chest that civilizations have been visiting Earth for millennia and it doesn't matter at this moment in time.

I'm here to execute the contract my soul signed before coming to earth and make sure I figure out what my purpose and essence are.

Instead of trying to figure out what the ancients knew, we should focus our efforts on growing spiritually and opening our Hearts to the planet and All Creatures who live here.

We should bless the earth as she continues to bless us.

I know nothing ... I'm being prepared ....

The more of the old belief system I discard, the more room I have for new inspired feelings and thoughts.

My preparation is none of my business. It's my job to surrender and accept the call with abandon!

> Today, I will unknow all I thought I knew
> as it no longer serves ME!

LIVE YOUR OWN DREAM, NOT SOMEONE ELSE'S ....

The journey to ME does not mean I go find a Guru and become a sheep.

Nor does it mean I hop off the escalator to pump life into someone's dream.

I believe each of us has a gift to share with the world.

Our growth stops once we get derailed onto the train tracks of someone else's dream or perception.

We have lost our way to Authenticity and Truth.

On my path, I feel the pull of others wanting to grab me during my ascension because they see my Heart and Energy can help further their dream.

It's not a bad thing and makes perfect sense, but if I am going to Truly find out what the Divine Creator is calling me to, I have to stay the course and trust that He/She has a plan.

I don't know what that plan is, but I feel I am doing Her will as I stay humble, keep quiet, and listen.

The messages come, and it's up to me to not discount them as something my brain made up because it does not follow the narrative I was programmed to follow.

When I am in surrender, and the voice speaks to me, I must answer the call now, even though I can't see where it is leading me.

I have complete faith and it is unwavering!

Very often, it is unpopular with those in my life, but I stay the course and follow my inner voice. No one knows what is best for me other than ME. A daily dose of SALT is required.

Today I will have blind faith and live in complete surrender, acceptance, let go, and trust!

REALIZING I HAVE THE POTENTIAL TO BE MY OWN MASTER ENABLED ME TO START THE ALCHEMICAL PROCESS OF BURNING OFF ALL THAT WASN'T SERVING ME ....

If they or it doesn't serve me, then they/it doesn't deserve me.

I cleared away All lower vibrational people (friends and family) that were not healthy for me.

They did nothing wrong, but I was allowing them into my life based on outdated programming that said I either owed them something or needed their approval.

People that don't serve my highest and best potential don't deserve to be close to me.

I had to learn to give love and compassion from a distance.

All attachments to worldly possessions and money had to be done away with in order for the Creator to begin downloading me with what He/She has planned for me.

All attachments to false identities had to be removed in order to become ME. I no longer have false pride, labels or titles. I don't say I am a Shaman, Healer or Master.... I simply exist as a being of the One Consciousness and Light we are all a part of.

No more blocking my Light and Energy with old, outdated relationships, beliefs, attachments, and habits. I don't allow anything that blocks my light from shining into my field!

Today, I will allow old me to fade into the distant past as I welcome the ME I was meant to be!

TO ME, WE LIVE IN HELL AND ITS MULTIFACETED FALLACIES ....

This is Hell here on earth and it is the survival of the fittest Souls.

We see and read about what hell is and what it looks like from false prophets and books written by men trying to control humans. But to me, we need to look no further than our own backyard.

We are in the Below battling like Hell in Hell to survive and evolve.

Look at the suffering here ... murder, rape, abuse, torture, neglect, hunger, power struggles, disease, greed, envy, jealousy, fear, sadness, trauma, children being gunned down at schools, natural disasters, fires, wars ... ad nauseum.

Our unhealed souls get to hang out here and hopefully awaken to their essence until it's time to reincarnate again.

The biggest battle in getting out
of Hell is within each of us.

We stay stuck in fear and anxiety when we believe what we see instead of manifesting our external reality from within.

We cannot evolve when our mind, body, and spirit are attached to the suffering of the 3D illusion created by the dark.

I feel the deeper we heal in each incarnation, the closer we get to our soul's highest level of consciousness!

How exciting that was to realize and it has fueled my desire to journey deeper and deeper into 'Who I Am!'.

Today, I will choose to see with my heart and not my mind as I wish to evolve to my highest self!

No Victims Allowed, and
That Includes Me ....

When I live from the 'Victim Stance', I spend my energy either feeling sorry for myself, blaming others, or trying to save others (Superman Syndrome) in order to receive love.

I used to be this unattractive bundle of self-loathing shame that would sabotage anything good that would come my way. My self-esteem was too low to accept a happy, healthy life. It just didn't match the trauma and upheaval I was used to as a child growing up. This is why the dark forces of earth indoctrinate our children from birth. They know if they can hardwire a child before age 7 or 8, they have them for most of their life. They create a world crisis in order to trigger the seeds they plant in humans as children.

I was the one dying inside as the cancer of
a false belief system kept me enslaved.

My coping skills kept me alive, but I made life miserable for myself and others. Am I being a big enough victim, so you will love me now? I used to tell my old story so people or women would feel sorry for me and love me. I had no authentic identity to draw from honestly. I didn't know WHO I Was!

I'll do more for you so you will love me more was how I loved. If these statements resonate within you, I encourage you to look at why you keep doing more and more for those you wish to receive love from. I realized I kept trying harder and harder and No One could ever match what I was giving so I felt like an even Bigger Victim as the energy wasn't being reciprocated.

I was actually digging the hole deeper as it worked in reverse.

> Today, I love who I am and know I deserve love, peace, and happiness!

My Story Became Like Toxic and Rotting Food ....

The romance of telling the sad story for attention wore off and I was just Ugly. I pushed away anything and anyone good in my life because it felt so foreign to me. In order to feed that feeling of worthlessness, I had to keep making decisions that held me hostage to the old story.

I would be a mess if my adult world didn't look like my childhood.

I'm grateful I finally got tired of looking in the mirror and only seeing my past, scars, wounds, traumas, the abandoned child, and shame!

As the Universe continues to transform me with my truth, I see how my old destructive patterns kept me in a spiritual prison.

Walking through my last divorce and knowing I wasn't running from anything but rather running to ME, took away all fear and anxiety around the decision. There was no way I was going to be able to answer this knowing in my chest within that container. I had to change one thing, Everything!

I see in the past that I would want to fill voids or fix myself by validation from a woman.

I would jump from relationship to relationship, taking hostages.

Today, I have no desire to use another futile effort to fix me.

I'm Not broken and have everything inside of me to heal and grow. As my intimate relationship grows with ME, I feel more love and support than any person, place, or thing could ever offer.

As a result, I feel my ability to love all grow, and I want to share that love.

> Today, I no longer rot from the inside
> out and let go of the story!

THE POWER OF SELF AFFIRMATION!

I don't look to be defined, I Am Infitinite.
I don't look for miracles, I Am a Miracle.
I don't look for the amazing, I Am Amazing.
I don't look for the answers, I Am The Answer.
I don't look For validation, I Am Valid.
I don't look for the divine, I Am Divinity.
I don't look for beauty, I Am Beautiful.
I don't look for the I Am, I Am the Great I Am.
I don't look for love, I Am Love.
I don't seek to master anything outside, I Am My Master!

I don't look for God, I Am God.
The YOU YOU Seek is within YOU

Today, I will honor and validate myself!!!!!!"

Setting Proper Boundaries Is Me Telling Me That I'm Worthy Of Being Loved And Supported ....

How do I show up for myself?

Showing up for myself before I try to show up for others is so important. I continue to get better at filling my cup before I try to love or support others.

When I show up for myself first, I can show Up for others from a place of self-love, compassion, safety, and authenticity. I must possess within what I am trying to give others.

I can't Love and Support others if I'm not loving and supporting ME.

Boundary setting helps me stay balanced and keeps energy vampires at a healthy distance.

I have an acute awareness today and can spot victims a mile away. They often want to latch on to my light instead of turning inward and doing their own work. I understand why they do this because I used to do it. Hopping on a guru's or self-proclaimed 'master's' coattail bypasses the journey meant for the individual.

My perception is that this will eventually fail you and you will seek another guru or master over and over in a repetitive cycle. This principle can be applied in all aspects of life with family, friends, and the work environment. "Blood, No Blood, No Difference!"

I don't owe a blood family member anything just because we are related.

Pay attention to how anxiety regarding people and circumstances subsides once you have loved yourself with a healthy boundary.

Today, I will Love others who don't belong
in my life from a healthy distance!

No Shortcuts!

There were no shortcuts to my Awakening. I had to do all of the messy, ugly work in order to be prepared to receive His/ Her Divinity which was planted deep within me, waiting to be activated.

I did some 15 years of psychotherapy before spending 4 years prior to my awakening with, what I call my spirit mothers, Nicole and Kadea.

I went deeper with them both than I knew I could or would be willing to go. I was Fearless in my efforts and completely Honest with them. I was painstakingly cleaning out my emotional closet leaving nothing hiding in the dark corners, nothing that could scare or hurt me anymore.

In Alcoholics Anonymous we say,
"half measures availed us nothing."

This has been true for me as I had to push all my chips to the middle of the table and go all in. Every deep dive into my wounds, traumas, neglects, abuses, abandonment, etc., was preparing me for my "Light to Ignite". Once I cleared the wreckage of my past, the light was clear to connect with my Creator's Will.

I realize now that my wounds and shadow seem healed, but much like an alcoholic's obsession to drink, I get a "daily reprieve based on the maintenance of my spiritual condition". Like a muscle, if I stop using or perfecting it, I'll lose it. My shadow is doing push-ups and waiting for me to step out of my light so it can lie to me with earthly desires, cravings, and short-term fixes.

Today, I choose love and I choose compassion... for my path and yours! Love yourself more today by doing the work!

GRATEFUL FOR HEALING MOMENTS! ....

Not long ago I got upset with my daughter Kennedy because it seemed to me that she kept slamming the car door and trunk. The loud noise kept upsetting me. As I intensley told her to stop slamming the door she would bark back at me thinking I was just getting upset over nothing.

I pondered why this was so upsetting to me. I went inside my heart and soul where my answers lie and it came to me. I was being triggered by the loud noise from childhood traumas that still have imprints within my cells.

I've done the work to heal these traumas but I now understand they are never completely gone.

There is always residue so there
will always be work to do!

Once I was able to realize where the trigger was coming from, I was able to apologize to Kennedy letting her know she hadn't done anything wrong, but rather the loud noise was triggering childhood traumas.

In turn, she showed compassion for me stating she was sorry it was upsetting me and would try to close them softer if it would help. She is aware I had a difficult childhood as I have shared my story with her.

I owned my part and apologized, and by doing so it allowed Kennedy to hear my Truth, validate it, and love me by showing compassion.

Kennedy is my favorite date and we recently saw Phantom of the Opera together.

I love her so much and she is one of my best friends, whether she knows it or not!

Today, I am grateful for the gift of introspection so I can see my part in all I do!

Calling BS on Myself ....

I love that I have enlightened guides lovingly following my progress and opening my mind further to the Bigger Picture I often can't comprehend. I quickly realize when I am full of shit and get my ego back in check.

As I am being given new information from across the globe daily, I have to remember my purpose in this incarnation is to heal my soul wounds. I came to heal and let the Creator show me the path I am to follow.

I'm not a Healer of others... I'm here to self-heal.

I'm not a teacher of others... I'm self-taught and lead by example (no one touched a hot stove for me when I was a child).

I'm not a guru suggesting I have your others... I am my own guru/master (with loving guidance from wise, enlightened beings).

I'm constantly being reminded to turn within and stop chasing ideas being planted in my head by human beings, cultures, media, and dark entities here on earth.

KISS (Keep It Soul Simple).

My spirit mother, Kadea, had me post "I Know Nothing" on my refrigerator to remind me I need to forget everything I've learned during this existence. I am being prepared for something The Mother wants me to do and I don't get to know what it is yet. The further I go, the less I realize I know. The reality is that the first 50 years of my life were a preparatory existence to awaken me for these times of Earthly and Human evolution.

Today, with love and grace, I will have compassion for ME!

The Medicine of Activation Breathwork! ....

During a Breathwork session months after my awakening, I was again transformed and blown open further!

During my journey, with the music blasting out tribal/ rhythmic music, I was being lovingly touched by one of the female facilitators when the call came strongly to me to ask her to "Bring Sonnie". Sonnie Dean was one of the facilitators there who I had never met before that afternoon. Spirit spoke to me saying I needed a Masculine presence.

Sonnie came to me with music blasting and a blindfold covering my eyes. As he put his hands on my heart and abdomen, I covered them with mine as we moved Energy together. He pushed harder on my chest and the pressure was intense. As he released, I grabbed him and pulled him down to me and we held each other intimately. I whispered in his ear, "I Love You" and "I See You", and kissed him on the neck. He whispered he loved me too and kissed me on the neck.

As I curled up in the fetal position afterward, I realized Sonnie helped me heal a father wound. My father, who was not my hero, used to want to kiss me as a sign of affection and I hated it. As I held Sonnie, I felt his closely shaven head and it reminded me of my now deceased father's head.

I'm not sure what that did for Sonnie but it was amazingly healing and deepening to my soul.

Upon our final embrace, we said goodbye, hugged, and kissed each other on the cheeks. Four hours together created a lifelong brotherhood between us.

Thank you Elaine Eagle Wolf for lovingly opening your home to the group that day in Dallas. You are such a gift and create a safe, sacred space for all and have a heart as big as Texas. I love you dearly! I love you Sonnie Dean!

Today, I will surrender to the process and have no expectation for what lies within my own breath!

No Preaching ....

Someone decided to preach God, Jesus Christ, and the Devil to me in a closed group. My reply went as follows:

Hi, and thank you for taking the time to reply.

I share what is working for me in my life and on my path and if anyone resonates with it, great.

I'm not looking to debate God or Jesus Christ or anything.

If your beliefs and perceptions are working for you, then I applaud you and your happiness.

I'm not selling anything or trying to convert Anyone.

There are 7.5 billion people on this planet and I only walk in My shoes. I only have the pen in my hand that writes My Story.

Your story and how you write it is none of my business.

I believe in a bit of everything as I am everything.

If I cling to one belief system or modality, I am separating myself from others and the universal consciousness of the All One.

I am a part of the collective Oneness is my belief. Religion and all of its restraints and shaming are not in alignment with ME.

If what I share does not resonate with you, please just move on until you find like-minded people in your tribe.

I believe if 7.5 billion people decided to look within themselves and do the messy work their souls came here to heal, all the world's "so-called" problems would melt away.

Today, I will live and let live from a place of non-judgment!

MY CHANNEL TO RECEIVE DIVINE LOVE HAS OPENED....

Now that the Creator's divine light has been ignited within me, I feel a deep sense of gratitude and responsibility to use it to guide others home. The Home Within!

As I continue to align my will with the Creator's, everything is making sense and my ability to see is expanding.

I no longer look through the foggy lens of false agreements and worldly domestication.

I can see clearly now, and all external desires have lost their flavor.

I only desire the Divine Nectar received when I am doing The Work of The One!

I have no fear of money!
I have no fear of being alone!
I have no fear of being accepted!
I have no fear of death!
I have no fear of being found out because I am my truth!

I finally see "Me" and I am beautiful just as I am... the Divine Truth I was seeking.

Nothing outside can touch me now as the Creator dwells in my heart and soul.

Today, I will honor the call and love all.

I HAD ALWAYS HELD THE WORLD RESPONSIBLE FOR UNMET EXPECTATIONS ....

Living and Loving from my wounds made me a victim, and I felt like the world Owed me a certain life.

When my expectations weren't met the way I thought they should be, I would stand up in my crib and bang my rattle until someone would feel sorry for me. I constantly felt let down and envious of others' lives, possessions, girlfriends, and the like. When am I going to get mine? That was a question I often asked of the universe.

Today, I know every unmet expectation
was a blessing in disguise.

Divinity was always at play and lovingly guiding me.

Had I got the 67' Camaro at age 16, it probably would have killed me in an accident.

Had I got the starting quarterback position I felt I deserved, it probably would have set my false ego on an even more destructive path than it was already on. Had I got the girl I wanted, I would have damaged her as I was incapable of loving correctly. Had I made more money, I would have just bought more alcohol and drugs that would have killed me. Had my parents stayed together, my mother probably would have been dead. Had I married the perfect woman for me, I would never have felt worthy enough for her and sabotaged the relationship.

Until I healed my wounds and let go absolutely to the divinity within me, I suffered and so did all those in my life.

When I set reasonable expectations on the world, I am much happier and I allow the Mother to determine the outcome knowing the thing or person I don't get is a blessing I can't always see.

It's None of My Business!

> Today, I will love myself more every day and the love I have for the world will endlessly expand!

Every Time I Changed the Girl, Where I Lived, Jobs, Friends, Circumstances.... I Kept Bringing Ocean With Me.

I kept dragging my shame, unworthiness, low self-esteem, traumas, wounds, etc., with me. I would start unpacking my shit from my suitcase of self-pity and making choices from my unhealed heart and soul. I kept wondering why I failed again.

The definition of insanity is doing the same thing over and over, expecting a new result.

I was insane to think I could make Anything work while trying to love and live from an unhealthy place.

I'm grateful for every choice as they have been the building blocks of the Being I continue to become, a being I truly love. I'm surrounded by my Tribe of people walking a spiritual path. I have had deeper relationships with them in 42 months than those I've had with family and friends I've known for a very long time.

I was walking on the beach in Carmel a while ago and saw a couple who looked so in love! Old me would have been envious and longed for that in my life. It would have triggered wounds of abandonment and loneliness.

I realized at that moment how much I had healed because I only had thoughts and feelings of pure joy and happiness for them. I realized I'm never alone anymore and the love I have for ME is enough.

My Queen will reveal herself to me in time, but that's not up to me and I'm not looking.

Today, I deeply love myself which means I deeply love you and present the highest and best version of me to all.

I HAD TO STOP FEEDING THE WILD ANIMAL THAT KEPT SHOWING UP AT MY BACKDOOR...

My story and the wounds associated with it stayed alive because I kept feeding them my energy and power. I was powerless because the story of my life had all of my power. If I keep feeding energy to my story, it keeps gaining strength and dominion over me. If I try to stuff it and ignore it, it just lays there doing pushups waiting for me to slip up.

My old story only has the
power that I assign to it.

The story stays alive from the negative, heavy energy I feed it... it's my fault. It sits on our shoulders weighing us down and keeping us in self-doubt, shame, and a seemingly hopeless state of mind and body!

I had no self-worth because I was afraid to stand up to my Old Story!

I am not validating myself and I am not loving and nurturing myself.

By giving my Story my power, I am allowing everything and everyone who ever hurt me to keep hurting me over and over and over again.

The Gifts of Desperation gave me the strength to stand up for myself and says, "I'm Ready to Take My Power Back!" I may not have been responsible for what happened in the past, but as an adult, it's my responsibility to own the fact that I was the reason it stayed alive and ruled my subconscious decisions.

I found it necessary to deal with every trauma, abuse, abandonment, and neglect I could think of. Ownership is the first step to recovery for a hopeless victim who feels the world owes him/her something. Wanting others to feel sorry for me was the only way I felt I could get them to accept and love me.

> Today, I will continue to slay the demons
> of my past and empower myself!

I Was Addicted to Suffering ....

It was and is a choice to Suffer.

I had to ask myself, "what suffering or things in my life do I choose to participate in today that do not resonate with my Authentic Truth?"

Of course, this meant I knew what my Truth was. Until I could connect with my higher self, asking this question was futile.

Once I did the necessary work that
allowed me to see my true self, I could
begin alchemizing my feelings, emotions,
and self-inflicted suffering into lessons
and opportunities for growth.

Otherwise, I was constantly paying the emotional debts I kept creating in order to mirror my old life as a child. I realize now I was addicted to the suffering of the familiar traumas and wounds still trapped and stored on a cellular level. Once again, I was a victim and a slave to the old story.

If deep suffering is the gateway to higher consciousness, then bring it on! Those who have fallen to the deepest depths can ascend to the highest levels of consciousness and states of Be-ing.

Being a victim and playing out the past in the present has no place in my life moving forward.

> Today, I will not allow my past to define my tomorrow!

I HAD THE KEY TO UNLOCK
THE ME I WAS SEEKING ....

We are born perfected beings of light, and then the key to unlocking our light is taken away and hidden in the deepest desert of the soul.

Life experiences build up and it is a journey to find that light again. We are sent here to Earth in Perfect Form and I allowed life on Earth and False Agreements to Imperfect ME.

The journey is a daily surrender
back to the perfected being of light
I once was and will be again.

I had to look in the mirror through the eyes of pure Love and tell myself, "You're Perfect exactly as you are." There are 7.5 billion stories being written at the same time.

Knowing the current You and your choices create the future 'You' is a great responsibility.

The consciousness we all belong to heals when each human heals and finds their way back home to their inner truth.

What is blocking you from diving deeper?
What traumas or wounds can you not look at?
What excuses do you attach to that keep you in revolving cycles?

We must ask ourselves these questions and begin the journey back to wholeness if we wish to be released from this soul prison called Earth. The "Key" lies in a place you would never think to look.....in your own heart!

Today, I will surrender and seek the key of life in ME!

I Don't Expect Much ....

Look deeply into my eyes ....
Softly hold the back of my head ....
Gently touch me ....
Hold my hand ....
Hug me often ....
Be my best friend ....
Be honest with me ....
Hold space for me without trying to fix me ....
Stay in bed just a bit longer in the morning ....
Wrap your arms around me from behind when I'm not looking ....
Kiss me in public and don't care about who is looking ....
Be still next to me and talk with your heart....
Allow me to dream ....
Lay your head on my chest and breathe ....
Laugh with me ....
Cry with me ....

Be the same person in the world that you are in my presence....
Carry the message of Love to the world with me ....

I only expect in return what I'm willing to give myself.
Love is the answer!

> Today, I'm willing to Love the way I wish to be loved!

Never Alone Again....

For me, as I continue to strive to embody love, I am no longer in search of it.

My marriage with my beloved Creator within and myself are enough. I no longer feel lonely or needy for someone.

I trust that it shall be done when the Creator wants to manifest her to me and it will be an expansion I've never known.

I have spoken to many trying to dream, manifest, or force the relationship they desperately desire.

I have no idea what day, month, or the year she will be brought to me. In the meantime, I busy myself with my divine purpose during this existence.

Bringing balance to the masculine and feminine energies on earth is embedded in my DNA, and I am passionately working to embody and model that!

I have surrendered and accepted this calling, and when it is time for a partner, she will appear. I have stopped looking as I know the time is not now. The Mountains, the birds, the oceans, the streams, the flowers, the animals, and the trees are my lovers and my teachers.

I am whole within, happy within, and never alone again.

Blessings and Namaste to Everyone's Journey Home Within.

Today, I know I am never alone and will shine my light for others to find their path home, so they never feel alone!

Now Vs. Then ....

Sometimes Ancient ideas, practices, beliefs, and ways of doing things need to be just that.... Ancient! Old! Expired!

Ancients practiced and believed the way they did because of the times they lived in.

If we are going to truly evolve in this day and age, we need to develop our own beliefs and practices that serve the greater good in current and future times. When we all build a belief system based on love and compassion for the earth and our fellow earthlings, we will create a land we could not imagine could exist.

We can honor and acknowledge the basic principles and simplicity of ancient wisdom without needing to go back and recreate things exactly as they did them.

That's why it's called Evolving! Things were different back then!

Life is more evolved and we have new wisdom that needs to coexist with ancient beliefs. We need to understand ancient wisdom as a complement to current wisdom in a relationship of balanced reciprocity.

Of course, this is just my perception.

Many philosophies, teachings, modalities, and religions see this very differently and bastardize the truth in order to gain further control of the human mind, heart, and soul.

> Today, I will engage in the evolution of all humans and Mother Earth by using my own inner wisdom.

DIVINE SOURCE

I offer myself to Thee,
To build with me and do
with me as Thou wilt.
Relieve me of the bondage of Self,
That I may better do Thy Will.
Take away my difficulties,
That victory over them
May bear witness to those
I would help of
Thy Power
Thy Love &
Thy Way of Life
May I do Thy Will always!

Third Step Prayer, Big Book of Alcoholics Anonymous.

And So, It Is ....

Today, I will continue to align my will with the Creator's will.

Teotihuacan Breathwork Training December 2019...

We Laughed
We Cried
We Argued
We Danced
We Journeyed
We Healed
We Rubbed One Another Raw
We Held One Another
We Kissed One Another
We Held Sacred Space
We Created a Safe Container
We Painted Together
We Climbed Pyramids
We Danced with our Shadows
We Married our Beloved
We Drank Bad Coffee
We Had the Best Host Family Ever
We Had the Best Facilitators
Most of All ... We Fell in Love!

Oh, And Sonnie Finally Landed His Eagle!!!
Inside Joke ... Love You, Sonnie Dean!

Today, I will remain open to new experiences
and offerings that expand ME!

Emotional and Spiritual Baggage ....

Much like a suitcase that weighs too much at the airport, I continued to pay the price when I dragged all of my emotional and spiritual baggage around everywhere I went.

Not only did I pay the price, but so did everyone in my life.

Until I became willing to look at The Man in the Mirror as the problem, I was stuck behind the mask of the false ego. The one that was blocking All of the Essence and Purpose I was meant to embody in this existence.

There was no magic pill, no magic workshop,
no magic plant medicine, no teacher, and
no guru that could solve my problems.

I was the problem and I was the one who kept feeding the wild animal (shame, victim, wounded child) who kept showing up at my back door every morning.

Doing my inner work, accepting my part, forgiving, letting go, and Complete surrender to the unknown nothingness of the stillness within took years. But the payoff has been transformational and transmutational. Letting go of everything not serving my higher self, released me from the bondage of the baggage I carried.

I love myself and have "sooo" much compassion for myself.

This allows me to give away what I now possess within and embody...

Pure unfiltered love and compassion for all beings, creatures, and the planet.

Today, I will no longer keep packing my emotional and spiritual baggage as I journey onward through life!

On this date, over 23 years ago, I looked in the mirror and hated who I saw.

I had become the man I swore I would never become, my father. Resentments and hate literally ate me alive from within as an evil and corroding thread throughout my energetic body.

I focused so much on who I didn't want to be that I actually called it in. I share my sobriety date to share my experience, strength, and hope with others so they may find the willingness to go to any lengths to overcome what is only a "Seemingly Hopeless State of Mind and Body."

We all need hope when we are bouncing off the bottom over and over and over. Just a mustard seed of Hope can get the worst I've seen to begin their journey. They need to hear and see in others what they are feeling and suffering, so they can relate enough to stop separating themselves and stay to do the work necessary to have a life beyond their wildest dreams.

Although I no longer struggle with wanting to drink, I still have a choice.

I have chosen over 8,400 times to not numb out with alcohol or drugs one day at a time.

I get a daily reprieve based on the maintenance of my spiritual condition.

> Today, I offer this message with all
> the love and humility I have.

WHO AM I WHEN NO ONE IS WATCHING? BECAUSE THAT IS WHO I TRULY AM! ....

When I am the person I am at home alone in front of the entire world, I am free! I have no secrets to hide, and I am Authentically just ME!!!

I no longer care what others think of me because I'm Not for everyone, and that's OK.

I don't please people out of fear of letting someone down or losing the relationship.

This morning I was walking my dog, and as usual, she pooped in a neighbor's grass. It was 5:30 am, still dark and no one was around. No one would know if I didn't pick it up, right?

But knowing I would know and I would hate it if someone did that to my yard, I picked it up and went on about my morning.

I build integrity by making choices that build self esteem whether someone is watching or not.

Integrity is who and what you say you are when you're alone and no one is watching.

Integrity is built when you are when you are alone with your-Self!

Food for thought.

> Today, I will live a life of integrity in all I do and not just when others are observing me!

DAILY INSPIRED MESSAGES COME IN THROUGHOUT MY DAYS ....

My messages and inspirations mostly come while driving, out running and on mountains.

I spend time discerning the Creator's messages and false ego messages. I try to keep things very simple and rest them just beneath my heart where my inner classroom lies. It is here I am able to feel true from false and gain awareness of the messages origin.

That is where my truth is, so that is where I send the messages.

I wait to Feel what resonates on a soul level as true for me.

I wait for the Feeling as I have stopped trying to think my way through things.

Things need to be very simplistic and I have everything I need inside me!

My mind, body and heart are my temples. My religion/philosophy is kindness, compassion and love! I don't derive my truth from a book or what others speak to me. I receive information and bring it inward. If it resonates as something I want to explore, I create an opportunity on the outside to gain experience which is then alchemized into wisdom.

> Today, I keep my mind open and my heart clear
> so I can receive the Creator's messages.

The Masculine Healing Needs to Happen in the Collective ....

As I journey and search for wisdom and enlightenment regarding the masculine wounding, it appears many of the men trying to help heal men base their offerings upon them regaining their masculine energy. Some retreats are based on getting in touch with physical strength, endurance, and even drinking alcohol.

I understand the need to bring those stuck in the divine feminine forward into the masculine, but it seems there is much more of a need to take the overly masculine men hiding behind their muscles and false ego into the light of their divine feminine in order to bring them back into balance.

The old Patriarchal Way of "I'm stronger than you" or "my penis is bigger than yours" has to go away.

Men will never be able to hold the Loving, Kind, Tender space women need until this has been done away with. Society paints a distorted picture, making it very difficult to undo this programming.

Until men understand the power of the divine feminine, they won't be able to take their proper place as her compliment .... Time to be done with this patriarchal Society and step into a new way of living, breathing, and loving.

Today, may the hearts of all be altered and softened to allow Her Divinity to guide us and the world.

As my Shaman Awakens, I am Realizing the Deeper I am Willing to Go the Less I Know ....

Everything I used to think was true was just a story I chose to believe. I was a parrot spitting out words that had been said to me, told to me, whispered to me, yelled into me, beaten into me, and shamed into me. I would say words as if I was right and therefore, you must be wrong.

Why? Because I had heard it from someone else, watched it on a TV show, heard it on the news, had an experience around it, and so on.

My truth has always been inside of Me
and it has nothing to do with you.

My soul and my "Inca Seed or Divine Light " had been asleep and now awake, my heart and inspiration has blown wide open.

I feel Love for everyone and everything because I am them and they are me.

Understanding I had to undo all I thought I knew was vital to my growth into ME. The conditioning in humans runs deep and it takes dedicated courage to break free from the illusionary false matrix.

We are All part of this incredibly divine ecosystem sent here to heal the soul and heal the Earth through pure light and love.

I always want to come from a place of love and share my feelings and what I am experiencing as my transformation continues to manifest itself. The alchemization of ones pain and suffering into hope and inspiration is available to us all.

Today, I will always remain open to new ideas and beliefs through new experiences!

LOVING FROM OUR WOUNDS ....

I can look back at my life and I see with crystal vision how I loved others with a broken heart and broken spirit. I was always trying to put my Superman cape on and save everyone from what had happened to Me. "Me" is the operative word.

How could I have thought I could save
anyone when I hadn't Saved Myself?

This was bypassing my own work. If I can find people I feel are broken and help them, I don't have to look in the mirror and fix me.

I was the one who needed to rescue my own heart and soul and the only way to do that was to keep diving deep inside of ME fearlessly. Until I healed and "Let Go Absolutely," my chances were nil! I Had to find the Divine within and begin to rebuild a relationship based on trust with my Creator and Me unconditionally. The Gifts of Desperation gave me the willingness to fearlessly face my demons before I was ready to guide others.

I have to have traveled to the depths of my soul and taken inventory of who I had allowed myself to become before I was ready to guide others there. I can't show you the way if I have not traveled the path myself.

I am now able to be the man I've always dreamed of. A true gatherer of souls and warrior of light.

I'm so happy and excited to meet those ready to take off their mask for good and be seen naked and raw. We are way more beautiful in our divine natural state.

> Today, I will no longer love others based on a past that no longer serves ME!

Hello Beautiful Soul ....

I See You
I Adore You
I Know You
I Accept You
I Believe in You
I Trust You
I Hear You
I Honor You
I Respect You
I Validate You
I Feel You
I Want You
I Need You
I Forgive You
I Love You

As I looked in the mirror and said these things to myself, I felt my heart expand and my ability to love all this way grew immensely.

Today, may we all be able to look in the mirror and love ourselves this way.

THE SHAMAN ....

The word 'shaman' comes from the language of the Evenk peo-
ple of Siberia who are known for their shamans. It means "the
one who knows" or "the one who sees in the dark" and has
healed oneself.

As western investigators became aware of these tribal vi-
sionaries, the word 'shaman' was chosen by anthropologists in
the last century to accurately describe the practices of tribal
mystics who were in service to their communities on a part-
time basis as healers and who had the ability to access the
Spirit World where they established relationship with spiritual
allies who assisted them in their endeavors to be of service.
The word 'shamanism' came into being to describe their arcane
practices.

Experience with Indigenous peoples says that 'authen-
tic shamans' actually never call themselves shamans. They
are called elders or Medicine People by others or sometimes
Shamans. In other words, the appellation is given to them by
their community based on their visionary abilities. They teach
by who they are—kind, respectful, honest, and humble.

The fasle new-age cultures have bastardized the word sha-
man and its meaning in order to fill their ego cups and profit off
those seeking healing. Keep in mind, there is nothing written to
draw truth from. The information has been orally transferred
down from generation to generation. Nonindigeonous people
speak about shamans and healers based on stories taught out-
side of the original tribes.

YOU are the Shaman as YOU have the ability to see and heal yourself.

Today, I am in touch with my inner Shaman and will bring him to the world in hopes I may guide others to heal themselves from within!

I'VE ALWAYS LOVED THIS SAYING, AND NOW I GET TO LIVE IT AS MY INNER SHAMAN HAS AWOKEN...

"I will be Fearless,
It will leave you Breathless,
Brace Yourself for Me"

We all have this in us! Awaken your Shaman and watch the world gasp for air in your presence! Then teach them how to breathe and awaken their inner Shaman!

Today, I will walk in truth and guide others to their truth!

Everyday Truth ....

I will no longer attach because when I get attached, I make someone or something an extension of me.

When that person or thing goes away, it feels like I'm losing a piece of me.

I will never give any part of ME away again.

I will walk and love from my authentic soul truth.

I will connect with life, people, creatures, and the Earth while continuing to love ME.

If I have to change who I am to "Make it Work,"
then it doesn't work. It is time to walk away
and not be afraid to let go so I can grow.

The same is true for someone else in my life. If they have to change who they are to try and "Make it Work," it just doesn't work.

I've worked on relationships for the past 28 years and I'm tired!

I will no longer look for love.

I will be love and let the Universal Creator guide me into and out of connections.

I now understand that each relationship has given me gifts and I am grateful for them all.

> Today, I will not allow fear of losing someone or something to keep me in unhealthy attachments!

I KNOW THE DIVINE MOTHER IS CALLING ME TO A GREATER PURPOSE THAN THE DOMESTICATED EXISTENCE I'VE TRIED TO LIVE...

Never knowing why life felt like such a struggle and why I could not find true inner peace, I was just existing and never truly living my truth and the divine purpose I was sent here for.

The light of The Mother residing inside me will no longer be in the dark corners of my heart buried by guilt, shame, abandonment, loneliness, insecurity, and fear.

I no longer have anxiety for my heart knows the truth of who I am.

I am a being of light sent here to help heal and teach those who want to receive.

I have ever expanded my love for this Earth and those who reside here.

I will no longer walk with my eyes wide shut while trying to live up to the expectations of this earthly conditioning.

I will spend the rest of my life writing my story from a place of Authenticity, Love and Compassion in hopes of drawing other's to their Light!

Today, I will be the change I want to see in the world.

As Above, So Below! ....

The struggle we feel is the programmed mind not wanting to Let Go of the illusion we have been force-fed since birth!

Your higher self (oversoul) is trying to get you to wake up and see through the veil of deception in order to bring forth your gifts so humanity may thrive with peace, compassion, and Love of all things. Lessons are constantly being sent to you in order for you to finally Surrnder and Accept your calling. The Gifts of Desperation will either pull you further into the abyss or you will finally be willing to receive that which has always been inside of you.

No longer be a "Consumer" of things you cannot take with you when you leave. When we buy unnecessary items, we have fallen victim to "The Program." The elites want us hooked on anything and everything in order to maintain control of humanity with money and debt. This illusion traps our minds and blocks the messages from the Creator to get through and into our hearts.

Remember, there is no separation in the Above. We are being force fed racisim and separation in order to keep us from creating more Love and Oneness. Spread your wings as the eagle or phoenix and rise above all you cannot see. Know that the only truth that matters is the one you were created to be!

Set yourself free and walk your Truth without fear of judgment and watch the seas part as your path magically appears.

Have the courage to say 'YES!' when the rest of the world would say 'NO!'. Be the change and the change will be!"

Today, I will let go of all I know in order
to be set free and know my soul!

IT'S NOT ABOUT GETTING BUSIER,
IT'S ABOUT GETTING QUIETER...

Being quiet is where I go to feel safe, loved, nurtured, creative, and happy. The only way I can get there is through stillness of all things. I had to learn how to shut down and quiet the mind that never wants to stop.

The mind is a programmed computer that
can be activated and turned on by what
we see, hear, feel, taste, and smell.

There have been activators installed throughout time within your own matrix and those activators are what ties anchors around your ankles holding you back from ascending into Who you were meant to be.

We all have a specific gift the world needs to experience in order to create cohesive peace and harmony on the planet and in the universe. The less we focus on the necessary changes within our own system, the more pain and suffering persist in the universe. I've learned to tap into The Universal Frequency Matrix that contains a frequency only I resonate with. When I'm in this space, No-Thing Matters or can touch me. I'm free to be ME without worry or concern of what others think.

Quieting the Mind stills my racing thoughts embedded and created by the outside world.

When I get quiet I can Hear the Divine Creators instructions. The ones specifically given to Me in order to bring forth my Essence and Purpose during this incarnation.

> Today, I will quiet the mind so I can hear
> my Heart and Soul's Calling.

CONSIDER THE HURT YOU FEEL THAT OTHERS CAUSED AS MOMENTS YOU YOURSELF CALLED IN AS SOUL AGREEMENTS TO PUSH YOU CLOSER TO SELF-LOVE...

I realize I called in all those who I thought hurt me. I feel I made agreements with my teachers and guides before I came to Earth. Incranation to incarnation, my soul has been evolving into higher states of consciousness. Each cycle were opportunites to reveal and heal what I came here for.

Relationships, careers, family, cultures, governments, religions, and friendships all offer opportunites to evolve in their own unique ways.

I need my father during this lifetime to play the role he played. I needed him to destroy me emotionally, mentally and physically as the final stages of my evolutionary process. I had been prepared lifetime after lifetime for this. The only way I could survive a childhood such as mine was because subconsciously and phsiologically I was at a point where giving up and numbing out were no longer options.

I now see my part in everything, and I'm no longer a victim. I needed everything to happen exactly as it did to be who I am today.

Today, I Am Grateful for All Things that brought me to the doorstep of Surrender and the Willingness to go to an lengths.

What is the Depth of Your Pain Threshold?

How spiritually, physically, and emotionally sick do you need to be to Surrender to the Necessary work that will give you the Happiness, Peace, Safety, and Love you long for?

Realizing your Existence
Recognition of your Truth
Reckoning with your Soul

Realizing the Feeling and Emotion
Recognizing why you're Activated and where it is coming from
Reckoning with that wound and taking your power back

Reveal It
Re-Feel It
Re-Heal It

I can't go home with you and make the changes YOU need to make in your life.

No one is coming to save you! Your Creator has given you everything you need to save yourself!

Today, I will step into the truth that I Am the Healer of M.E.!

FINDING AND SPENDING TIME WITH MY SPIRIT FAMILY, IGNITES AND INSPIRES MY SOUL'S ESSENCE AND PURPOSE.

My Earth family served me in a way that got me to humility and surrender. I'm deeply grateful!

However, I needed to find and connect with my Spiritual Family in order to evolve and expand. I began reading books such as "The Untethered Soul" and "The Alchemist" in order to seek guidance and expansion. The more I fed my soul the greater the frequency of truth I emenated from my being. This emenation created a vibrational pull that was magnetic. People began showing up to offer guidance, love and support in ways I was not familiar with.

Send out your highest and best vibration today and watch the world change just by raising your own consciousness and begin creating your outer reality from deep within.

This is an inner journey specific to You and surrounding yourself with your cosmic family/tribe can ignite the fires of who you're here to Be-Come.

Surrender to your innermost truth and transmute anything and anyone blocking you from getting there.

One Tribe
One Heart
One Breath
One Love

Today, realize Your Truth by finding your
tribe that will help set you free.

Progress Not Perfection!

I'm not as Great as I'm Going to Be,
But I'm Way Better Than I Used to Be.

~ Ocean Eagle ~

Upcoming Books, Courses, and Retreats

- *The Gifts of Desperation, A Journey Back to M.E.*
- *Mind Stirring Business Secrets w/ Kevin Harrington*
- *The Gift of Inspirations, Vol 2*
- *The Gift of Inspirations, Vol 3*
- *The Cosmic Soul, Where Science Meets Spirit*

As the founder of Activation Breathwork, Ocean Eagle will be launching the online course in 2023. He will teach people everything about this deep journey into subconscious belief systems binding humanity to suffering and revolving, unhealthy cycles.

He will also offer in-person Facilitator Certification opportunities for those called to dive deeper. Ocean offers many in-person 5–10-day retreats in Sedona, AZ, Mexico, Peru, and other amazing locations. There are Men Only, Women Only and Co-ed.

Go to:

Www.OceanEagle.Org

Www.ActivationBreathwork.Com

www.authoroceaneagle.com

Register your email address on his main website
to be notified of all Ocean is offering.

Printed in the USA
CPSIA information can be obtained
at www.ICGtesting.com
LVHW011935221123
764286LV00002B/6